A Guide to Monastic

GUEST HOUSES

A Guide to Monastic
GUEST HOUSES

THIRD EDITION

Robert J. Regalbuto

MOREHOUSE PUBLISHING

Morehouse Publishing
P.O. Box 1321
Harrisburg, PA 17105

Morehouse Publishing is a division of Morehouse Group.

First Printing, 1998

Printed in the United States of America

Cover photograph of All Saints Convent (Episcopal), Catonsville, Maryland, by Leslie Everheart.

Cover design by Corey Kent.

Artwork by Jennifer Bailey appears on pages 1, 3, 5, 7, 11, 17, 19, 23, 25, 31, 35, 45, 47, 49, 53, 55, 57, 63, 65, 69, 71, 79, 93, 99, 101, 103, 105, 107, 113, 117, 119, 123, 127, 133, 137, 143, 147, 153, 157, 161, 163, 167, 169, 171, 175, 177, 185, 187, 189, 191, 195, 197, 201, 203, 207, 211, 217, 219, 221, 225, 233, 239, 241, 243, 245, 249, and 253. Other illustrations by B. Griffiths.

Library of Congress Cataloging-in-Publication Data
Regalbuto, Robert J.
    A guide to monastic guest houses / Robert J. Regalbuto. — 3rd ed.
      p. cm.
    ISBN 0-8192-1713-1 (pbk.)
    1. Hotels—United States—Guidebooks. 2. Hotels—
Canada—Guidebooks. 3. Monasteries—United States—
Guidebooks. 4. Monasteries—Canada—Guidebooks. 5. United
States—Guidebooks. 6. Canada—Guidebooks. I. Title.
TX907.2.R44   1998
647.9473'01—dc21   97-38227
                                       CIP

To
my mother

May Louise S. Regalbuto

1925–1988

with

love and gratitude

Contents

Acknowledgments

I am most grateful to the nuns, monks, and others who have graciously provided hospitality to me, and to those without whose cooperation and information this book would not have been possible. Many of the monastics have expressed thanks to me for the *Guide*. Rather, it is for me to thank them. Even more so I thank those who have offered prayerful support to me and to this work.

Thanks are due also to my brother, Joseph Regalbuto, Jr., for his interest and thoughtful suggestions for the book's content. No acknowledgment would be complete without a particular word of gratitude to Deborah Grahame, former senior editor at Morehouse Publishing Company. For a decade and through three editions of this *Guide* I have had the benefit of her expertise and professionalism, and for that I am most thankful.

Once again I wish to extend special thanks to John Hinman, M.D. I am indebted to him for his advice and commentary on nearly every aspect of the book, and for his generosity in giving many hours of his time to reading and offering editorial comment on the manuscript.

Preface

Tempus fugit, and such is the case with *A Guide to Monastic Guest Houses*. It was ten years ago, in 1987, that I took up my pen to write the first edition. Two editions and a decade later I am pleased to write that the *Guide* has been widely read and continues to lead readers to places of rest, refreshment, and spiritual renewal. Since the first edition the book has grown. At first offering representative guest houses throughout the United States, the second edition had the addition of Canadian convents and monasteries. As I have traveled and researched further, I am happy to present a third edition that includes every state of the Union and all Canadian provinces. As in previous editions, detailed, practical information is given for the guest houses as well as "interesting vignettes about each locale," as *Spiritual Book News* put it. The book continues to have a wide Christian denominational representation, presents a spectrum of monastic traditions and observances, and offers settings that run the gamut from urban Midtown Manhattan to the most remote corner of the New Mexico desert. And each of the guest houses opens its doors to those of other faiths. In short, *A Guide to Monastic Guest Houses* is broad in its appeal rather than narrow, a guide for the many rather than the few.

It would be shortsighted to use the *Guide* as a resource for budget accommodations. Remember when reserving time for a private retreat that the guest houses in this book are a ministry of the communities that offer the pilgrim not only room and board, but spiritual sustenance as well. However, it should be noted that a survey was conducted among the guest houses. In nearly every reply, the monastics responded that they will offer spiritual direction *to those who request it*. If this is your wish, it should be mentioned when reservations are made. In writing about the *Guide*, the *National Catholic Reporter* so aptly put it: "Here is an alternative for people who like vacations that heal, are truly restful and economical."

The practical information at the beginning of each listing is meant to help the guest when contacting the monastery or convent for reservations. The charges quoted are current at the time of writing but subject to change. (Canadian charges are given in Canadian dollars.) It is advisable to book as far in advance as possible. Some guest houses are so popular that booking well ahead is not only advisable but necessary.

An excellent approach for the newcomer at a monastery guest house is to remember that a monastic community is a *family* and that, like every family, it has its own traditions, customs, and rules. But no need to worry—monasteries are used to newcomers and guests. The Guest Master or Guest Mistress, other community members, and/or guest literature will help familiarize you with house rules so that you can settle in comfortably and enjoy your stay.

The author is most heartened by letters from nuns, monks, and the readership in general in response to the first two editions of the *Guide*. Some have offered suggestions for additional guest houses, and I have followed up on these. May the *Guide* continue its mission to lead you, the reader, to a "place apart" where monastic hospitality is offered and a "holy leisure" enjoyed, giving that peace "which passeth all understanding."

Woodside Cottage
Newport, Rhode Island
14 May 1997

Numbers here correspond to the page where the guest house entry appears in the guide. See Contents (page vii).

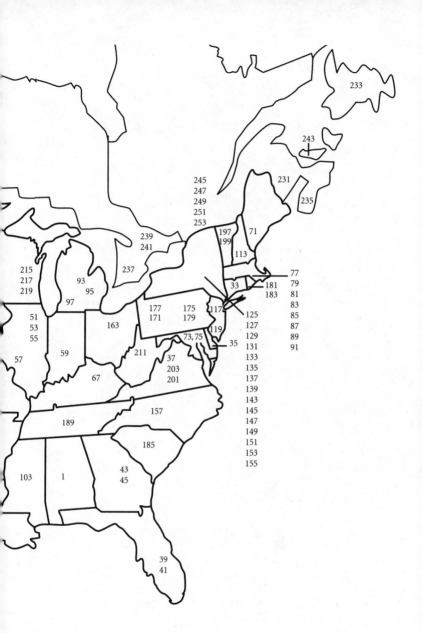

United States

Sacred Heart Monastery

Benedictine Spirituality and Conference Center
Post Office Box 488
Cullman, Alabama 35056

Telephone: (205) 734-8302. (Best time to call: Monday through Friday 9:00 A.M. to 5:00 P.M.)

Facsimile: (205) 734-8302 (by appointment).

Order: Benedictine sisters (Roman Catholic).

Accommodations: Up to sixty-nine guests in single, twin-bedded, and triple-bedded rooms, all with shared baths.

Meals: Three meals daily.

Charges: $30 for room and $15 for meals per person per day.

Write, telephone, or fax: The Director.

1

Directions: If driving from Birmingham, take I-65 north to Exit 308 and continue east on Route 278. At Convent Road, turn left at Route 278 (traffic light) and go to the second gate on the right. Parking is on the right; building entrance is behind the statue.

For those using public transportation, there is Greyhound bus service to Cullman. Please contact the Director for further directions.

History: There has been a Benedictine presence in Alabama since the 1860s when monks arrived from Pennsylvania. Later that century Benedictine sisters arrived and opened Sacred Heart Monastery. At the turn of the century the expansive and impressive Gothic Revival monastery and church were built.

Description: Outside the monastery guests may want to explore the two-hundred-acre property and its gardens. Nearby is St. Bernard's Abbey, home to forty monks. The abbey church is a study in contrast of architectural style as compared with that at Sacred Heart Monastery. Sacred Heart's church was built in traditional medieval Gothic style with appropriate details, while the church at St. Bernard's provides a more modified and modern interpretation of the same architectural principles.

Points of Interest: While visiting St. Bernard's Abbey, be sure to see the Ave Maria Grotto. Lovingly built by a monk long ago, the grotto is, surprisingly, one of the most popular tourist attractions in Alabama, a major link in the "Bible belt."

Special Note: The Benedictine Spirituality and Conference Center publishes a full schedule of special programs, a copy of which is available on request.

The Lodge at the Shrine of St. Therese

5933 Lund Street
Juneau, Alaska 99801

Telephone: (907) 780-6112. (Best time to call: 8:00 A.M. to 5:00 P.M.)

Order: Founded by Jesuits (Roman Catholic).

Accommodations: Up to twenty-three guests in the lodge in ten rooms, all with shared baths. There are also three log cabins: one with a kitchenette and private bath, the other two being quite rustic with wood-burning stoves and outhouses.

Meals: Please contact the Director regarding meals.

Charges: Rates are variable. Please contact the Director in this regard.

Write or telephone: The Director.

Directions: Drivers can find the shrine located on Mile 23+ of the Glacier Highway north of Juneau.

If using public transportation, contact the Director for directions.

History: A Jesuit priest, Fr. William LeVasseur, was inspired to found the shrine in the 1930s. His dream became a reality when, in 1941, he celebrated an inaugural mass in the shrine's chapel.

Description: The chapel is on its own island, accessible by a 400-foot-long pedestrian causeway. Two bishops, Joseph Crimont (Alaska's first bishop, who died in 1945) and Michael Kenny (died in 1995), are interred in the chapel's crypt. Both the chapel and the outdoor Stations of the Cross are built of beach stones from the property. Using the self-guided tour brochure provided, feel free to explore the forty-six acres of the shrine, its buildings, and its natural beauty. On the shores of Lynn Canal, the majestic Chilkat Mountains provide a serene backdrop to the shrine. It is not unusual to spot salmon, whales, sea lions, and soaring eagles when touring the property.

Points of Interest: A place of stunning and spectacular natural beauty, Juneau offers visitors glaciers and other natural wonders of Alaska.

Holy Trinity Monastery
Post Office Box 298
St. David, Arizona 85630

Telephone: (520) 720-4016 or 720-4642. (Best time to call: Monday through Saturday 9:00 A.M. to 4:00 P.M.)

Facsimile: (520) 720-4202.

Order: Benedictine monks (Roman Catholic).

Accommodations: Eleven men and twelve women in the guest houses in single and twin-bedded rooms, some with private baths.

Meals: Three meals daily.

Charges: $30 per person per day for room and meals.

Write, telephone, or fax: Dr. Benedict Lemki, O.S.B., the Guest Master.

Directions: If driving from Tucson, take Highway 80 fifty-eight miles southeast to the town of St. David.

For those using public transportation, there is air service to Tucson and Greyhound bus and Amtrak train service to Benson (nine miles away). Please contact the Guest Master for further directions.

History: The Roman Catholic Bishop of Tucson, wishing to have a Christian Renewal Center in Cochise County, invited Benedictine monks to his diocese in 1974. Fr. Louis B. Hasenfuss of the Benedictine Abbey in Pecos, New Mexico, was joined by two young men. Within two months of their arrival ground was broken for Our Lady of Guadalupe Church. The church was completed and dedicated in 1981. In 1992 the Bureau of Land Management helped dedicate a 1.3-mile-long bird sanctuary trail.

Description: The church is inspired by the Pueblo style so prevalent in the American Southwest. Both church and monastery are situated on ninety-three acres bordered by the bird sanctuary trail. "HTM," as the monastery is often called, has an oriental garden, an RV park, a bookstore and gift shop, Gallery Trinitas (a museum and art gallery), and Benedict's Closet (a thrift shop). The Whetstone Mountains form a breathtaking backdrop west of HTM. An interesting aside: the San Pedro Valley Center for the Arts is housed at HTM, with ongoing workshops in painting, sculpture, pottery, and other art forms. Through an affiliation with the Arizona Commission on the Arts and Cochise College, many concerts are presented to the public at HTM.

Special Note: HTM's program is unique in that this is a residential community of monks, sisters, and laity who live the Benedictine ideal. Further, HTM has about 750 lay oblates across the United States and abroad. HTM is ecumenical in its outreach.

Servants of Christ Priory

28 West Pasadena Avenue
Phoenix, Arizona 85013-2002

Telephone: (602) 248-9321.

Order: Benedictine monks (Episcopal).

Accommodations: Five guests in single and twin rooms, two of which have a private bath.

Meals: Three meals daily.

Charges: $40 per day for room and meals.

Write or telephone: The Guest Master.

Directions: If driving on I-17, take the Camelback Road exit going east at Third Avenue, turn north one block and then east on Pasadena Avenue to the priory.

If driving on I-10, take the I-17 turnoff and proceed as directed above.

If you are using public transportation, the Super Shuttle will take you from the airport to the priory door. There is bus service and Amtrak passenger rail service to Phoenix. If additional directions are needed, please contact the Guest Master by letter or phone.

History: Founded in 1968 as a community of priests and laymen, the apostolate of the Servants of Christ Priory is to be a monastic witness in an urban environment. The current priory property was acquired in 1989.

Description: The priory offers a place of silence and refuge within the city of Phoenix. An attractive brick building, the priory is surrounded by trees, and numerous potted plants greet the visitor at the front door. The Chapel of the Transfiguration and the adjoining guest house are set back at the far end of the property. There is also a bookstore where prayer books, hymnals, Bibles, icons, religious jewelry, candles, altar bread, inspirational books and tapes, and greeting cards are sold.

Points of Interest: Of particular interest to guests may be the Prayer Garden (at 9849 North 40th Street) maintained and opened to the public by the Evangelical Sisterhood of Mary. The Sisterhood is a Lutheran community founded in Germany following World War II.

Phoenix is the heart and capital of Arizona. The city has a number of museums, the Heard Museum being most noted for its impressive collection devoted to Arizona's history, Indian culture, anthropology, and art. The Desert Botanical Garden, Encanto Park, Pueblo Grande, and South Mountain Park are also nearby. Scottsdale is close to Phoenix. Sedona, Montezuma Castle, and the Grand Canyon National Park are north of the city and the priory.

Coury House

Subiaco Abbey
Subiaco, Arkansas 72865

Telephone: (501) 934-4411.

Facsimile: (501) 934-4040.

Order: Benedictine monks (Roman Catholic).

Accommodations: Sixty-one guests in one single, three double, and twenty-seven twin-bedded rooms.

Meals: Available in the guest dining room.

Charges: Available upon request.

Write, telephone, or fax: Brother Mel Stinson, O.S.B., Guest Master.

9

Directions: By car, Subiaco Abbey and Coury House are located 125 miles west of Little Rock. Take I-40 West to Exit 55. Follow the signs.

From Fort Smith, travel on Highway 22 forty-eight miles east to Subiaco.

If you are using public transportation, Fort Smith airport is recommended. Please contact the Guest Master for further directions.

History: St. Benedict established a monastery at Subiaco, Italy, in the sixth century. Thirteen hundred years later an American Subiaco Abbey was founded in 1878 by monks from St. Meinrad's Abbey, Indiana, to minister to the needs of the German immigrant population in Western Arkansas and Texas. The monks of Subiaco established parishes, schools, and, in 1963, Coury House—a guest and retreat center to offer a quiet place for prayer, reflection, and spiritual directions for those seeking "a place apart."

Description: The abbey church, modified Romanesque in style, was completed in 1959. Of special note are the 182 German stained-glass windows depicting episodes in the life of St. Benedict. The church, bell tower, and cloister are all constructed of native sandstone. Spacious and well-manicured grounds surround the abbey. Here one may explore the walking and hiking paths, meditative areas, a grotto, beautiful gazebos, and out-of-doors Stations of the Cross.

Points of Interest: Majestic Mount Magazine is 20 miles south of Subiaco. Post and Wiederkehr Wineries, and historic St. Mary's Church in Altus, are located 35 miles from the abbey.

Special Note: A descriptive brochure and further information are available from Br. Mel Stinson, the Director and Guest Master.

Incarnation Monastery

1369 LaLoma Avenue
Berkeley, California 94708

Telephone: (510) 845-0601. (Best time to call: 9:00 A.M. to 5:00 P.M.)

Facsimile: (510) 548-6439.

Order: Camaldolese Benedictine monks (Roman Catholic).

Accommodations: Four guests in the monastery in two single rooms and one twin-bedded room, all with shared baths.

Meals: Breakfast.

Charges: $30 suggested donation for bed and breakfast.

Write, telephone, or fax: Br. Cassian Hardie.

Directions: If driving north on Highway 80, make a right on University Avenue, a left on Oxford Street, and a right onto Cedar Street. LaLoma Avenue will be on your left.

If using public transportation, take BART (subway) to the Downtown Berkeley Station. The AC Transit #8 bus stops in front of the monastery.

History: Two men have had key roles in the history of the Camaldolese. The first was St. Benedict (sixth century), the Father of Western Monasticism and the founder of the Benedictine Order/family of which the Camaldolese are a part. The second was St. Romuald who, in eleventh-century Italy, revitalized a part of the order at Camaldoli, infusing it with a vocation expressed in two life styles: that lived in community and that of a hermit. In 1958 the Camaldolese arrived in America and established a monastery at Big Sur, California. Incarnation Monastery, a house of studies, was opened in the 1990s.

Description: Each guest room has a separate entrance and its own balcony with a beautiful view of the entire San Francisco Bay. Adjacent to the monastery is a very pleasant public park.

The main campus of the University of California at Berkeley is just a few blocks from the monastery, and the Graduate Theological Union is close by. The GTU combines nine seminaries (Episcopal, Baptist, Lutheran, Presbyterian, Unitarian, Interdenominational, and three Roman Catholic). Orthodox, Judaic, and Buddhist institutes are also located in the area.

Points of Interest: Berkeley and the Bay Area offer numerous opportunities for cultural experiences in such areas as music, dance, and literature. As the monks at Incarnation Monastery suggest, "Why not re-create yourself with a cultural retreat linked to the prayer and hospitality of the monastery?"

Incarnation Priory

1601 Oxford Street
Berkeley, California 94709

Telephone: (510) 548-3406.

Order: Order of the Holy Cross (Episcopal).

Accommodations: Up to four guests may be accommodated in three rooms, all with shared baths.

Meals: Not available.

Charges: $35 per person per night.

Write or telephone: The Guest Master.

Directions: The Guest Master will provide directions on request.

History: The Order of the Holy Cross, the oldest religious order of men in the Episcopal Church, was founded in 1884. Incarnation Priory was opened by the Order of the Holy Cross in 1973.

Description: The priory is in an urban setting a very short distance from the Graduate Theological Union.

Points of Interest: The University of California at Berkeley is close to the priory, and San Francisco is only thirty minutes away.

Special Note: Most of the monks work and study in the area during the day, returning to the priory in the evening. Guests are always welcome to join the monks at morning and evening services in the Chapel of St. Augustine and St. Gregory.

Mount Calvary Retreat House

Post Office Box 1296
Santa Barbara, California 93102-1296

Telephone: (805) 962-9855.

Order: Order of the Holy Cross (Episcopal).

Accommodations: Thirty guests in eight single and eleven twin rooms with private or semiprivate baths.

Meals: Three meals daily.

Charges: $60 per person per day for room and meals.

Write or telephone: The Guest Master, Br. Antony Pisner, O.H.C.

Directions: If coming by car, request directions.

For those using public transportation, there are plane, train, and bus services to Santa Barbara. Arrange in advance to be met.

History: This house of the Order of the Holy Cross was established in 1947 by Fr. Karl Tiedemann, O.H.C. Mount Calvary was opened to serve as the order's retreat house and conference center on the West Coast.

Description: The retreat house was built in the style of a large Spanish house. It is dramatically situated on a ridge 1,250 feet above the city of Santa Barbara. Mount Calvary enjoys commanding views of the seacoast and the Pacific Ocean.

Special Note: Group retreats are given at Mount Calvary. Contact the Guest Master for a brochure and further information.

Mount Tabor Monastery
Post Office Box 217
Redwood Valley, California 95470-0217

Telephone: (707) 485-8959. (Best time to call: 8:00 A.M.)

Facsimile: (707) 485-1122.

Order: The Monks of Mt. Tabor (Ukranian Catholic).

Accommodations: Fourteen guests in the guest house in ten single and two twin-bedded rooms, all with shared baths.

Meals: Three meals daily (according to monastic diet and fastings).

Charges: In summer $25 per person per day, in winter $35 per person per day, for room and meals.

Write, telephone, or fax: The Guest Master.

Directions: If driving from Highway 101, just north of Highway 20 take the West Road exit and continue on to Tomki Road. The monastery will be on your right about one mile after the road goes up the hill.

There is no public transportation available.

History: In the early 1970s, following a long and distinguished academic career on three continents, Archimandrite Boniface Luykx founded Holy Transfiguration Monastery at Mt. Tabor in the Redwood Valley. The founder, now in his eighties, is Mt. Tabor's abbot as well as a world-renowned liturgist, theologian, and expert on Eastern Christian spirituality.

Description: Mt. Tabor includes 240 heavily wooded hillside acres. The monastery, designed and built in traditional Ukranian architectural style, is of timber and topped with domes and crosses. The monks, nearly a dozen in all, each live in individual ten-by-twelve-foot houses. Apart from the village of monks and farther up the hill is the retreat house. Guests may wish to explore the network of fire roads that cross Mt. Tabor.

Points of Interest: The Redwood Forest is located nearby. Within its groves of ancient trees are some of the world's tallest.

Prince of Peace Abbey
Oceanside, California 92054

Telephone: (619) 430-1305 and 430-1306.

Facsimile: (619) 967-8711.

Order: Benedictine monks (Roman Catholic).

Accommodations: Thirty-four guests in the guest house in ten single and twelve double rooms, each with private bath.

Meals: Three meals daily.

Charges: Donation of $35 per person per day for room and meals.

Write, telephone, or fax: Fr. Sharbel Ewen, O.S.B.

Directions: By car from Interstate 5, exit State Route 76. Go east on State Route 76 to Benet Road. Make a left on Benet Road and left again on the next road. This will take you over a one-lane bridge. The sign directly in front points to the road on the right. Follow this road to the top of the hill.

From Interstate 15 (traveling north or south), exit at State Route 76 and travel west on 76 about seventeen miles through the town of Bonsall and continue on to Oceanside. Exit right on Benet Road. The first road on the left takes you over a one-lane bridge. The sign directly in front points to the road on the right. Follow the road to the top of the hill.

If traveling on State Route 78, exit El Camino Real and continue north, turning left (west) on Mission Avenue until you get to Benet Road. Exit right on Benet Road, then take first road on left over a one-lane bridge. The sign directly in front points to the road on the right. Follow this to the top of the hill.

For those using public transportation, there are bus and Amtrak services to Oceanside. Contact the Guest Master for further directions.

History: Prince of Peace Abbey was founded in 1958 by monks from St. Meinrad's Archabbey, Indiana.

Description: The abbey, its monastery, church, and guest house are located about one hundred miles south of Los Angeles and thirty-five miles north of San Diego. They are situated on a hill overlooking San Luis Rey River Valley and the Pacific Ocean.

Points of Interest: The Mission San Luis Rey, dating from 1798, is near the abbey.

St. Andrew's Abbey

31001 N. Valyermo Road
Post Office Box 40
Valyermo, California 93563

Telephone: (805) 944-2178.

Order: Benedictine monks (Roman Catholic).

Accommodations: Thirty-four guests in seventeen twin-bedded rooms in the guest house, each with private bath.

Meals: Three meals daily.

Charges: Suggested donation of $45 to $50 per day per person for room and meals.

Write or telephone: The Guest Master.

Directions: By car from Los Angeles, take Route 14 to Pearblossom Highway exit. Go down Longview Road and then left onto Avenue W, which becomes Valyermo Road.

By public transportation, take Greyhound to Lancaster or a train to Acton. Contact the Guest Master for further details.

History: St. Andrew's Abbey traces its roots to the Belgian Abbey of St. Andrew. Belgian monks were sent to China in 1929, and when expelled by the Communists in 1952, the community resettled in Valyermo in 1955. From the beginning, monastic hospitality has been a work of the monks here, and in 1958 a new guest house was opened.

Description: Valyermo is in the Mojave Desert just northeast of Los Angeles. The abbey's buildings, contemporary in design, are set in a wooded area. The abbey is known worldwide for its ceramics, and these are exhibited and sold at the Monastery Art and Gift Shop at the abbey. Stations of the Way of the Cross are placed along the hillside here.

Special Note: The abbey sponsors workshops, group retreats, and days of recollection. Contact the abbey's Guest Master for further information and literature.

St. Francis House

3743 Cesar Chavez Street
San Francisco, California 94110

Telephone: (415) 824-0288. (Best times to call: 4:30 P.M. and 7:40 P.M. to 8:30 P.M.)

Facsimile: (415) 826-7569.

Order: Community of St. Francis (Episcopal).

Accommodations: Two guests in one twin-bedded apartment with private bath.

Meals: As requested.

Charges: $30 per day for room.

Write, telephone, or fax: The Guest Sister.

Directions: If driving from downtown, take Highway 101 south to Cesar Chavez Street exit. Then go west on Cesar Chavez Street just past Guerro Street.

If driving from the airport, take Highway 280 to the San Jose exit. Go past the first stop light, then turn left on Dolores Street. Continue nine blocks to Cesar Chavez Street. Turn right. St. Francis House is in the middle of the block.

If you are using public transportation, take the "J Church" streetcar to the 27th Street stop. It is then a two-block walk to St. Francis House. Alternately, take BART (subway) to 24th and Mission. It is then a ten-minute walk to the house.

History: The Community of St. Francis is a part of the Anglican Franciscan Society of St. Francis. The community was founded in 1905 in England, and its members live a life of prayer, study, and work among the poor and marginalized.

Description: St. Francis House is a fine example of a 1930s San Francisco Art Deco-style house. The guest apartment, on the first floor, overlooks a garden. St. Francis House is an urban community house, located in the historic Mission District near San Francisco's Hispanic neighborhood.

Points of Interest: Often referred to as "everyone's favorite city," San Francisco has some exceptionally beautiful cathedrals: Grace Episcopal Cathedral on Nob Hill (Gothic Revival), St. Mary's Roman Catholic Cathedral (strikingly modern), and the onion-domed Holy Virgin Russian Orthodox Cathedral. The Old Mission Dolores, Chinatown, Golden Gate Bridge and Park, Fisherman's Wharf, and Alcatraz are also popular sites.

St. Mary's Retreat House

505 East Los Olivos
Santa Barbara, California 93105

Telephone: (805) 682-4117. (Best days to call: Weekdays other than Thursdays.)

Order: Sisters of the Holy Nativity (Episcopal).

Accommodations: Twenty-five guests in single and twin-bedded rooms in the guest house, all with shared baths.

Meals: Three meals daily.

Charges: $65 per person for a two-night stay including six meals.

Write or telephone: The Guest Mistress.

Directions: If driving from points north or south, take Highway 101 and exit at Mission Street in Santa Barbara. Turn toward the mountains on Mission Street and follow the signs to the Old Mission. St. Mary's driveway is the second left after the Mission.

If you are using public transportation, there are air and Amtrak services to Santa Barbara, and then taxi service to St. Mary's. If arriving on Greyhound bus, go next door to the city bus terminal. The city bus labeled "Old Mission" will take you to within walking distance to St. Mary's.

History: The Sisterhood of the Holy Nativity, founded in Boston in 1882, later moved to Fond du Lac, Wisconsin, and opened St. Mary's Retreat House in 1954. Its purpose is to provide a place for people to "come away from the crowd and spend time alone with God."

Description: St. Mary's has two large houses, an English half-timber chapel, and other small buildings. There are a good library and a comfortable living room for the use of guests. The extensive grounds have many walks and gardens with nooks and crannies, a terrace, an outdoor altar, and outdoor Stations of the Cross.

My soul doth magnify the Lord,
    and my spirit hath rejoiced in God my Savior.
For he hath regarded the lowliness of his handmaiden.
For behold, from henceforth all generations shall call me blessed.
For he that is mighty hath magnified me,
    and holy is his Name.
And his mercy is on them that fear him
    throughout all generations.
He hath showed strength with his arm;
    he hath scattered the proud in the imagination of their hearts.
He hath put down the mighty from their seat,
    and hath exalted the humble and meek.
He hath filled the hungry with good things,
    and the rich he hath sent empty away.
He remembering his mercy hath holpen his servant Israel,
    as he promised to our forefathers,
Abraham and his seed, for ever.

— The Magnificat, The Book of Common Prayer

The Retreat House

Immaculate Heart Hermitage
Big Sur, California 93920

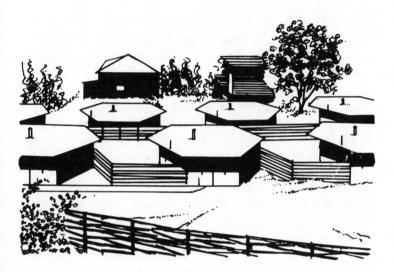

Telephone: (408) 667-2456.

Order: Camaldolese monks (Roman Catholic).

Accommodations: Nine guests in the monastery and guest house, each in a single room with toilet and washbasin. Showers are shared. In addition, there are five trailer-hermitages on the hermitage grounds accommodating one guest each.

Meals: Three meals (vegetarian) daily.

Charges: $45 per person per day for room and meals in the Retreat House, or $55 per person per day ($335 per week) for trailer-hermitages.

Write or telephone: The Guest Master.

Directions: The hermitage is located at Lucia, off the Coast Highway (California Route 1), about twenty-five miles south of Big Sur and fifty-five miles south of Monterey. The hermitage entrance road, on the inland side of the highway, is marked by a large brown wooden cross.

If taking a plane or bus to Monterey, guests can be met (by prior arrangement) on Friday afternoons between 5:00 and 7:00 P.M.

History: The Camaldolese hermits, founded by St. Romuald near Arrezzo, Italy, in 1012, are a reform within the Order of St. Benedict. The hermits may lead either a solitary life or a life in community. New Camaldoli was opened at Big Sur in 1958.

Description: The hermitage is on a five-hundred-acre tract of land in the Santa Lucia mountain range. The Camaldolese have always favored the eremitical life-style, and guests will find every opportunity for solitude here. The guest rooms have views of the Pacific Ocean.

Special Note: The length of stay for guests in the monastery is from three days to one week. The length of stay for guests staying in one of the trailers-hermitages is three days to one month. Preached retreats on a theme are given five or six times a year. The schedule for the following year is published every fall. Literature and further information are available from the hermitage's Guest Master.

Holy Cross Abbey

Post Office Box 1510
Canon City, Colorado 81212-1510

Telephone: (719) 275-8631, Ext. 212.

Order: Benedictine monks (Roman Catholic).

Accommodations: Up to seventy-one guests in forty-two rooms (single and twin) in the guest house and Hedley House, all with shared baths.

Meals: Three meals daily.

Charges: Rooms are $14; breakfast is $4; lunch is $5; and dinner is $7. The total is $30 per person per day for room and three meals.

Write or telephone: Larry Winker, Manager of Operations.

Directions: The abbey is located on U.S. Highway 50, two miles east of Canon City and thirty-eight miles west of Pueblo.

For public transportation, there is Greyhound bus service to Canon City.

History: Benedictine monks arrived in Colorado in 1886 and after several moves, settled in Canon City in 1924. Just two years after the monks arrived in Canon City, the present monastery, chapel, and library were completed. Built of brick and granite, the handsome Gothic Revival buildings were placed on the National Register of Historic Places in 1983.

Description: The monastery, guest houses, and community center (with its gift shop) are located within the more than two hundred acres owned by the abbey. Over half of this acreage is utilized as farmland.

Points of Interest: The Royal Gorge is in Canon City, and visitors can enjoy "river rafting" on the Arkansas River. Restored Western towns and mines are here and in the neighboring town of Cripple Creek. In nearby Colorado Springs are the U.S. Air Force Academy, the Space Control Center, and the beautifully landscaped Garden of the Gods. Colorado City is home to the Olympic Training Center, the Rodeo Hall of Fame, and the restored Ghost City.

Special Note: The abbey offers group retreats in addition to welcoming individual guests. Contact the abbey's Guest Master for further information. Guests are cordially invited to attend and participate in the daily monastic services.

St. Benedict's Monastery

1012 Monastery Road
Snowmass, Colorado 81654

Telephone: (970) 927-1162 (guest house) and (970) 927-3311 (monastery).

Order: Cistercian (Trappist) monks (Roman Catholic).

Accommodations: Two guests in the gatehouse, each in a single room and both with shared bath. In addition, there are twin beds for two people in the barn apartment. Up to sixteen guests may be accommodated in eight self-contained units (with kitchenette and bath) in the new retreat center.

Meals: Guests prepare their own meals.

Charges: There is a suggested donation of $30 per person per night for room and meals.

Write or telephone: The Guest Master.

Directions: If driving from Denver, take I-70 to Glenwood Springs, then Highway 82 from Glenwood Springs to Old Snowmass, which is two and a half miles past Basalt. Turn right at the intersection where there is a Conoco gas station. Then go straight for about seven and a half miles, bearing right at the one crossroad. At the end of seven and a half miles you will see a sign for the monastery on the left side of the road. Turn left at the sign onto the monastery road and travel one mile to the gatehouse, which is next to a large wooden arch spanning the road.

For those using public transportation, there is air service to Aspen. Amtrak trains and Greyhound buses go to Glenwood Springs. Arrange with the Guest Master in advance to be met at the airport, depot, or station.

Description: Set in a valley at an elevation of 8,000 feet, St. Benedict's Monastery property is extensive and includes a ranch, streams, hills, aspen forests, and meadowlands. The monastery abuts a national forest, and the nearest neighbors (none closer than a mile) are ranchers. The monks work on their own ranch and in their greenhouse. The new retreat center has a chapel/meditation hall, a library, conference rooms, a kitchen, and a dining room.

Special Note: Groups of up to ten guests may stay in the ranch house in twin rooms with shared bath. The ranch house is usually booked several months in advance. A descriptive brochure is available from the Guest Master.

Convent of St. Birgitta

Vikingsborg
4 Runkenhage Road
Darien, Connecticut 06820

Telephone: (203) 655-1068.

Order: Sisters of St. Birgitta (Roman Catholic).

Accommodations: Twelve guests in the guest house in single and twin rooms, all with private baths. In addition, six guests may be accommodated in three twin rooms in the cottage.

Meals: Three meals daily.

Charges: $80 single, or $140 double, per day for room and meals.

Write or telephone: Sr. Sabina.

Directions: By car from New York, New Jersey, and southern Connecticut, take the Connecticut Turnpike to Exit 12; turn right onto Tokeneke Road. Proceed a half mile on Tokeneke Road to intersection island; bear right around island to Old Farm Road and follow a half mile to Tokeneke Trail. Bear right on Tokeneke Trail and proceed a half mile to Runkenhage Road (note green shield-shaped sign on the left of road). Turn onto Runkenhage Road to first driveway on the right (about fifty feet from turn); drive through two sets of stone posts in direction of sign reading "Vikingsborg."

By public transportation, take the New Haven Railroad to Darien, Connecticut. Taxis are available at the station at each train arrival. The convent is about 1¾ miles from the station.

History: The patron and namesake of this order is St. Birgitta of Sweden, a Swedish noblewoman born in 1303 and widely known in medieval times through the reading of her *Revelations.* The Order flourished in northern Europe during the Middle Ages but nearly became extinct following the Reformation. The sisters began an era of resurgence and growth early in the twentieth century, and in 1957 four sisters arrived in Darien to take up residence at Vikingsborg.

Description: The spacious guest house is close to woodland walks and gardens, and guests enjoy "the peace, silence, serenity, and beauty which surrounds the whole place..."

Points of Interest: Vikingsborg is on the Long Island Sound.

Special Note: The convent does not schedule retreats, but retreat groups of all denominations are welcome to come with their own director for days of recollection, meditation, study, discussion, or workshop. Literature and information are available from the convent's Guest Sister.

St. Francis Renewal Center
1901 Prior Road
Wilmington, Delaware 19809-1398

Telephone: (302) 798-1454.

Facsimile: (302) 798-3360.

Order: Capuchin Franciscan Friars (Roman Catholic).

Accommodations: Eighteen guests in nine twin-bedded rooms in the retreat house, all with shared baths.

Meals: Three meals daily.

Charges: Please contact the Center for charges.

Write, telephone, or fax: Father Thomas Pietrantonio, O.F.M. Cap.

Directions: Please contact the Center for directions by car and by public transportation.

History: It was St. Francis of Assisi who would withdraw from the busy hill town of Assisi to a place known as "I Carceri." This was his retreat and hermitage. His followers, the Franciscans, grew in number and spread throughout Europe and beyond beginning in the thirteenth century. In 1529 a reform within the Franciscan order began. This new group of friars became popularly known as "capuchins"—a name based on the word origin of the hood they wear. Today Capuchin Franciscan friars, in the spirit of their founder St. Francis, provide a retreat for those who seek it. In a sense, St. Francis Renewal Center is another "I Carceri" for many.

Description: This is a century-old mansion that has been refurbished and transformed into a comfortable retreat. Located on the outer edge of the city of Wilmington, the Center is surrounded by greenery and nature.

Points of Interest: North of Wilmington are the Winterthur Museum and Longwood Gardens in the picturesque Brandywine Valley.

Special Note: Guests should remember that St. Francis Renewal Center is a place of spiritual retreat, whether they are there for a day of recollection or for a longer stay. Visits to nearby points of interest and similar activities should be scheduled for either before or after one's retreat.

St. Anselm's Abbey

4501 South Dakota Avenue, N.E.
Washington, D.C. 20017

Telephone: (202) 269-2300.

Order: Benedictine monks (Roman Catholic).

Accommodations: Eight men in the monastery in single rooms, most with shared bath. "Men with a spiritual purpose are welcome for brief visits."

Meals: Three meals daily.

Charges: An offering of $25 per day for room and meals is suggested.

Write or telephone: The Guest Master.

Directions: For public transportation, take the Metro to Brookland-CUA (Red Line), then any R bus to South Dakota Avenue and Michigan Avenue. Cross South Dakota Avenue and walk one block to the abbey gates.

History: In 1923 five Americans, intent on living as Benedictine monks in Washington, went to the Scottish Abbey of Fort Augustus. The following year, after completing their novitiate training, they returned to Washington with several monks from Fort Augustus and established St. Anselm's in a wooden farm-house on a tract of land not far from the Catholic University of America. In 1930 the monks moved into a newly built English Tudor-style monastery. A newer, more modern wing was added in 1964. A day school for boys was opened in 1942.

Description: The red brick abbey church with its wooden choir stalls and stained-glass windows is the nucleus of the abbey property. The abbey's grounds are a peaceful refuge within urban Washington.

Points of Interest: The abbey is close to the Catholic University of America, the Basilica of the National Shrine of the Immaculate Conception, and the Franciscan Monastery with its Holy Land shrine/replicas. The Washington Metro system provides fast and easy access to Washington National Cathedral and other points of religious, cultural, educational, and historic interest.

Holy Name Monastery

Post Office Box 2450
33201 Highway 52 East
St. Leo, Florida 33574-2450

Telephone: (302) 588-8320.

Order: Benedictine Sisters of Florida (Roman Catholic).

Accommodations: Sixteen guests in single rooms in the monastery, all with shared baths.

Meals: Please arrange with the monastery for meal service.

Charges: $20 per person per day for room. Meals are $15 per day if taken at the monastery.

Write or telephone: The Program Coordinator.

Directions: If driving on I-75, take Exit 59 and go east on Highway 52 for approximately three miles.

From I-4, take Exit 18 and go north on Highway 98 to Highway 52 (thirty miles).

If using public transportation, the nearest airport is Tampa International Airport. There is also Greyhound bus service to Dade City. Please contact the Program Coordinator for more information.

History: In 1889 the settlers of Florida's Catholic Colony of San Antonio invited the sisters from Pennsylvania. Five of the sisters opened Holy Name Academy. The monastery now numbers thirty members.

Description: Located on one hundred acres of gently rolling hills, the monastery is a modern building overlooking scenic Lake Jovita. This quiet and peaceful area, with palm trees surrounded by orange groves, extends into the adjoining property of St. Leo's Abbey and St. Leo College. Recreational facilities here include a swimming pool, tennis courts, and a golf course.

Points of Interest: Walt Disney World, Busch Gardens, the John F. Kennedy Space Center, Cypress Gardens, and other sights are an hour or so from the monastery.

Special Note: In addition to welcoming individual guests, the monastery also offers group retreats. Please contact the Program Coordinator for more information.

St. Leo Abbey

Post Office Box 2037
St. Leo, Florida 33574

Telephone: (904) 588-2881 or (904) 588-2009.

Order: Benedictine monks (Roman Catholic).

Accommodations: Up to sixty guests in thirty rooms (single and twin) in the guest house, some of which have private baths. In addition, there are some rooms available in the monastery. Please contact the Guest Master for more information.

Meals: Three meals daily.

Charges: $32 per person per day for room and meals.

Write or telephone: The Guest Master.

Directions: If driving on Interstate 75, take Exit 59. State Road 52 goes right by the abbey.

For those using public transportation, there are bus and Amtrak train services to Dade City. There is air service to Tampa International Airport, and from there limousine service to the abbey (or arrange with the Guest Master in advance for pickup).

History: History began at St. Leo Abbey in 1889 when monks from Belmont Abbey, North Carolina, arrived in Central Florida. They established a military school, then a preparatory school, and, in 1959, St. Leo College. Today the community numbers about sixty members, many of whom are from a variety of cultural backgrounds, adding much to the present chapter in the abbey's history.

Description: The abbey church is popularly known as the church "that was built with orange juice," as the cost of its construction was largely defrayed by income from the abbey's citrus groves. It is Lombard-Romanesque in design, its wooden appointments made from the abbey's cedar trees. A 2,100-pound marble crucifix is the focal point of the sanctuary. Guests may use walkways unhurriedly through fifty acres of woods along the lakefront. Beyond is some of the most beautiful countryside in Florida.

Points of Interest: Florida's beaches are but an hour from the abbey, and Walt Disney World, Universal Studios, and the Salvador Dali Museum are each an hour and a half away. Busch Gardens is forty minutes away. The John F. Kennedy Space Center is a 2½-hour trip from here.

Special Note: In addition to receiving individual guests, St. Leo's also offers group retreats. Please contact the Guest Master for more information.

Convent of St. Helena

3042 Eagle Drive
Post Office Box 5645
Augusta, Georgia 30916-5645

Telephone: (706) 798-5201.

Facsimile: (706) 796-0079.

Order: Order of St. Helena (Episcopal).

Accommodations: Eleven guests in single rooms. Most rooms have shared baths.

Meals: Three meals daily.

Charges: Freewill offerings accepted.

Write, telephone, or fax: The Guest Mistress.

Directions: Driving directions given on request.

If using public transportation, there are plane and bus services to Augusta. Arrange in advance to be met on arrival.

History: The Order of St. Helena was founded in Kentucky in 1945. In 1961 the Bishop of Georgia invited the sisters to open a house in his diocese. Given a gift of more than eleven acres of land in Augusta, the sisters first lived in a log cabin here. In 1965 ground was broken for the present convent and chapel.

Description: Contemporary design and the use of concrete, wood, and glass have given the convent a feeling of simplicity and spaciousness. On the property are oak and pine trees that the sisters planted soon after their arrival, as well as flowering shrubs, benches, ponds, birdhouses, and an altar in the woods. Located on a partially wooded hill just south of Augusta, the convent has views of the city's skyline and of South Carolina across the Savannah River.

Special Note: Open conducted retreats and workshops are periodically given at the convent. Information about these activities may be obtained from the Guest Mistress.

Monastery of Our Lady of the Holy Spirit

2625 Highway 212
Conyers, Georgia 30208

Telephone: (770) 760-0959. (Best times to call: 10:00 A.M. to 12:00 noon and 2:30 P.M. to 4:30 P.M.)

Facsimile: (770) 760-0989.

Order: Cistercian (Trappist) monks (Roman Catholic).

Accommodations: Forty guests in the retreat house in single rooms, all with shared baths.

Meals: Three meals daily.

Charges: $35 per person per day for room and meals.

Write, telephone, or fax: The Guest Master.

Directions: If driving from downtown Atlanta, take Interstate 20 east to Exit 37. Turn right onto Panola Road and go 2.3 miles to the fourth traffic light. Turn left onto Brown's Mill Road (Route 212). Then continue nine-and-one-half miles to the monastery, which will be on your left.

For those using public transportation, the Shuttle Service (at telephone number 770-922-5083) will pick up at Atlanta Airport, train, or bus station with advance notice. Another option from Atlanta Airport is the train to Five Points Station. At the station, transfer to #86 Marta bus. At Lithonia, get off at Wendy's. Call the Shuttle Service in advance for pickup there.

History: Honey Creek Plantation was bought by the monks in 1944. At first living in a barn loft, with hard work, prayer, and imagination, the monks transformed the former plantation into an abbey complete with church, bell tower, and cloistered quadrangle.

Description: About thirty miles from downtown Atlanta, the abbey is a place of austere beauty and solitude. The abbey church, of modified Gothic design, has a quiet, serene interior lit by rows of stained-glass windows. It took a quarter of a century to build and complete the abbey.

Points of Interest: Stone Mountain and the city of Atlanta are in the area.

St. Isaac's Hermitage

Post Office Box 731
Mountain View, Hawaii 96771

Telephone: None.

Order: Hermits of St. Benedict (The American Orthodox Church).

Accommodations: Four guests in two cabins, each with a double bed, portable toilet, and sink. There is one central shower. Each cabin also has its own chapel.

Meals: Food for breakfast and supper are provided and self-prepared. A cooked meal is served midafternoon.

Charges: $35 per day per room, single occupancy, and $50 per room per day, double occupancy.

Write to: Father Louis Fair, O.S.B.

Directions: Please contact Fr. Louis regarding driving directions when reservations are made. If you are using public transportation, rides can be arranged to and from Hilo Airport.

History: St. Isaac's Hermitage was founded in 1994 by Archbishop Louis W. Fair. This was the fulfillment of a twenty-five year dream. He was joined by Mother Gabriella, Deaconess and Prioress, and together they began their joint project with $800 and prayer. At first they cleared 125 feet of rain-forest jungle, built a deck, and there pitched tents. The tents in time were replaced by a village of small cabins, each surrounded by thick foliage to assure the solitude sought here.

Description: Located on the Island of Hawaii, the hermitage is 2,500 feet above sea level in an isolated rain forest. The forest has been left as natural as possible—with no decorative floral beds, blacktop roads, or concrete sidewalks. "We are deliberately primitive," says Fr. Louis. "Above all, we offer a serious, primitive, contemplative environment. We do not pretend to be a luxury vacation resort. There are plenty of those in these Islands! St. Isaac's is not for spiritual dilettantes."

Points of Interest: The entrance to Volcanos National Forest is ten miles from the hermitage. Within the forest are active lava flows, including spectacular flows from Kilnea Crater to the ocean.

Special Note: This is a tropical rain forest, so guests should dress accordingly and be prepared for heavy rain, very hot days, and cold nights, any of which can occur year-round. The nearest telephone is seven miles away, and the monastics "hope to keep it that way." When writing for reservations, please keep in mind that the hermits suggest a minimum stay of seven days and that a 30 percent nonrefundable deposit is required.

Marymount Hermitage

2150 Hermitage Lane
Mesa, Idaho 83643-5005

Telephone: (208) 256-4354 (messages only).

Order: Hermit Sisters of Mary (Roman Catholic).

Accommodations: Three guests in single or double occupancy in hermitages, each with private bath.

Meals: Three meals daily (self-prepared in the hermitages).

Charges: $20 for room and $15 for meals per person per day.

Write to: Sister M. Beverly, H.S.M.

Directions: For those driving, Marymount Hermitage is located west of Highway 95, between Council and Cambridge, midway between mile markers 128 and 129, just north of the Mesa town site. (Be sure to arrive before sunset as there are no streetlights in the area.)

For those using public transportation, there is air service to Boise (2½ hours away), train service to Ontario, Oregon (1½ hours south), and bus service to Boise, Ontario, and New Meadows, Idaho (one hour north). A neighbor of the hermitage, with prior notice and for cash payment, can provide a car service from these towns for the following fees: Boise, $75 round trip; Ontario, $45; and New Meadows, $30.

History: The eremitical (i.e., hermit) tradition in Christian monasticism is centuries old, inspired by the lives and teachings of the Desert Fathers. With a reverence for this tradition and an authentic spirit of renewal, Marymount Hermitage was solemnly dedicated in 1984. At first Marymount included three hermitages, a chapel/library, and a common house. In 1987 the bell tower rang its first peal, and two additional hermitages were built the following year. "Our Father's House," the new chapel, was dedicated in 1994.

Description: On one hundred acres of rolling, high desert rangeland, Marymount is at an elevation of 3,200 feet. Surrounded by mountains, the hermitage itself is on a mesa overlooking a valley 200 feet below. Look for wildlife such as birds, rabbits, and deer. There are also coyotes, small rodents, snakes, and lizards, which the sisters assure us are "harmless."

Special Note: "We send out a free quarterly newsletter to explain the spirituality and material progress of Marymount Hermitage."

Bethlehem House

Convent of St. Anne
1125 N. La Salle Boulevard
Chicago, Illinois 60610-2601

Telephone: (312) 642-3638.

Order: Sisters of St. Anne (Episcopal).

Accommodations: Five guests in single rooms, all with shared bath.

Meals: No meals for individual guests on private retreats.

Charges: Please contact the Guest Mistress in advance for charges.

Write or telephone: The Guest Mistress.

Directions: Contact the Guest Mistress if driving directions are needed.

For those using public transportation, the nearest subway stop is at Clark and Division.

History: The Order of St. Anne was begun by a Cowley Father, the Reverend Frederick Powell, in 1910 in Massachusetts. The order grew to include houses in a number of states and countries, where the sisters had undertaken a variety of charitable works.

Description: Bethlehem House is a small island of tranquility in the midst of downtown Chicago. The house is in the virtual shadow of the Church of the Ascension. The parish has been at the forefront of the Anglo-Catholic movement in the Episcopal Church since 1869.

The present limestone church, at the corner of La Salle and Elm, was built in 1881. Clearly, the focal point of the interior is the high altar that dates to 1894 and is embellished with English alabaster statues and Venetian mosaic panels.

Points of Interest: Other noteworthy churches in the immediate area include the Victorian Gothic Cathedrals of St. James (the oldest Episcopal church in Chicago) and Holy Name (Roman Catholic). Ralph Adams Cram's English Perpendicular Gothic masterpiece, the Fourth Presbyterian Church, is on Michigan Avenue. Other historic churches, sites, and museums are also in the Loop.

Chicago Priory of Christ the King

4334 N. Hazel Street #110
Chicago, Illinois 60613

Telephone: (773) 404-2767. (Call between 9.00 A.M. and noon, Central Standard Time).

Order: Benedictine Brothers/Oblates (Episcopal).

Accommodations: Two men in the priory, each in a single room with private bath.

Meals: Self-prepared in the kitchen or sometimes shared at a local inner-city restaurant.

Charges: $25 per person per night.

Write or telephone: The Guest Brother.

Directions: The priory is at the corner of Montrose Street and Broadway. If driving, contact the priory for directions.

Public transportation is available "but is not advised for persons new to the inner-city because of the high crime rate."

History: The Chicago Priory and its sister ministry in Australia have an apostolate of promoting biblical discipleship under the Benedictine Rule. The priory has a special concern for both competent biblical scholarship and practical "hands on" ministry to the urban poor. It has been established since 1985 and is in its canonical formation period. The Priory has a strong affiliation with the neighboring Church of the Atonement.

Description: The priory maintains a small library and chapel for study and prayerful meditation. It also supports work projects for inner-city shelters, parishes, and persons in need. In accordance with the Rule, both brothers and guests are required to work in some form of constructive labor, as well as spend time in study and spiritual exercises.

Special Note: Only directed retreats are scheduled, and these are usually integrated with the special liturgical services of Christmas, Epiphany, Lent, and/or Easter. Contact the prior for details. The brothers request that sightseeing in Chicago be reserved for either before or after the retreat itself.

Monastery of the Holy Cross

3111 South Aberdeen Street
Chicago, Illinois 60608-6503

Telephone: (773) 927-7424.

Facsimile: (773) 927-5734.

Order: Benedictine monks (Roman Catholic).

Accommodations: Eleven guests in seven single and two twin-bedded rooms in St. Joseph's Loft or the Coach House, all with shared baths.

Meals: Three meals daily. Breakfast is served in the guest houses; other meals are eaten with the monks.

Charges: Suggested offering of $35 per person per day.

Write, telephone, or fax: The Guest Master.

Directions: If driving from the Dan Ryan Expressway (Interstates 90 and 94), take Exit 54 (31st Street exit) and go west. The monastery is located at the corner of 31st and Aberdeen Streets. Landmark: this is the second church steeple west of the Expressway. Alternately, from Lake Shore Drive (Highway 41) take the 31st Street exit. The monastery has the third church steeple west of Lake Shore Drive. Off-street parking is provided in a secure lot.

For those using public transportation, Midway Airport is the closer airport (fifteen minutes away). O'Hare Airport is an hour away. From either airport take the train to the Halted Stop on the Orange (Midway) Line. With advance notice you may be picked up at this stop, which is one mile from the monastery. Or you may transfer to the 62 Archer Bus heading west (go to the bus stop at curb directly in front of the train station) and get off at Loomis Street. Walk south two blocks on Loomis Street to the monastery church.

History: It was in 1991 that the late Joseph Cardinal Bernadin invited this Benedictine community to Chicago to take up residence at the former Immaculate Conception Church (which had been closed a year earlier). The monks have transformed the former parish church building, rectory, convent, and other facilities into a vibrant urban monastic center. Holy Cross has a close affiliation with the Monastery of Christ in the Desert, New Mexico.

Description: The monastery church is a century-old massive Gothic Revival structure. The spacious interior, lit by some of the finest stained-glass windows in Chicago, is furnished with a delicately carved wood reredos and hand-painted icons. Outside the church there is a walled cloister garden that guests find particularly inviting.

Points of Interest: The monastery is located in the Bridgeport neighborhood just south of the Loop. This is an ethnically and racially diverse area with a great variety of shops and restaurants. Close by is the McCormick Place Convention Complex, and the White Sox Park is just ten minutes away. Chinatown is also nearby. Just down the street (at the east end of 31st Street) is Lake Michigan with its swimming beaches and extensive walking and biking paths. Farther afield, it is a fifteen-minute bus ride to downtown Chicago with its numerous points of religious, cultural, and educational interest.

St. Benedict Abbey

7561 West Lancaster Road
Bartonville, Illinois 61607

Telephone: (309) 633-0057. (Best times to call: 9:00 A.M. to 12:00 noon and 3:30 P.M. to 5:00 P.M.)

Facsimile: (309) 633-0058.

Order: Benedictine monks (ecumenical).

Accommodations: Please call Dom Luis for current information.

Meals: Three meals daily.

Charges: $30 per person per day for room and meals.

Write, telephone, or fax: Very Rev. Dom Luis Gonzalez, O.S.B., Prior and Administrator.

Directions: If driving from Peoria, take I-74 west as if going toward Galesburg. Take Exit 87A (I-474 Indianapolis). Continue on I-474 for about four miles and take Exit 5 (Airport Road). At the stoplight make a left. Drive on Airport Road (airport will be on your right) for about two miles. Make a right on Pfeiffer Road;

Limestone High School will be on the corner. Lancaster Road springs out of Pfeiffer Road toward the left. Drive for about a mile and a half, and the monastery will be on your right.

For visitors using public transportation, there is air service to Peoria. For those flying to O'Hare Airport, the Peoria Charter Coach Company has a shuttle to Bradley University in Peoria at a cost of $24 one way. In either case, arrange in advance with Dom Luis for pickup on arrival in Peoria.

History: St. Benedict Abbey may be the most recently opened monastery in America today. Its roots are in Puerto Rico, where the community was founded in 1985 by Dom J. Alberto Morales. With a great deal of faith and courage, the monks transferred their abbey from Puerto Rico to Illinois in 1996. The budding community suffered many hardships after their arrival. But, as one of the monks relates, "God always sends angels to meet us." The people of Illinois have welcomed and helped the monks; the monks in turn have ministered to the local community. Yet the struggle to reestablish the abbey in the United States is far from over. With prayer, hard work, good planning, and much-needed help from friends, the monks hope to expand the monastery, its guest facilities, its church, and its life, work, and witness.

Description: The abbey is located in a quiet, pastoral setting surrounded by rolling fields. The generosity of benefactors is reflected in the newly planted evergreens donated by a friend and a nursery. One of the monks writes, "They were planted for the greater glory of God and to create a contemplative environment for our abbey so that our visitors may enjoy privacy and contact with nature—God's creation."

Points of Interest: Peoria is home to the Forest Park Nature Center, the Wildlife Prairie Park, and the George L. Luthy Memorial Botanical Gardens. Museums include the Lakeview Museum of Arts and Sciences and the Wheels of Time Museum. Illinois, the "Land of Lincoln," has sites related to the president's life in Springfield, the state capital, just seventy miles south of Peoria.

Special Note: St. Benedict Abbey is truly ecumenical in spirit and in outreach and welcomes all to its new home.

St. Meinrad Archabbey Guest House
St. Meinrad, Indiana 47577

Telephone: (812) 357-6585.

Order: Benedictine monks(Roman Catholic).

Accommodations: Forty-six guests in twenty-one twin-bedded and four single rooms, each with private bath.

Meals: Three meals daily.

Charges: Rooms are $27 per day, single occupancy, and $32 per day, double occupancy. Meals are approximately $13 per day.

Write or telephone: The Guest Master.

Directions: Located on I-64, the abbey is seventy-five miles from Louisville, Kentucky, and fifty-five miles from Evansville, Indiana.

For those using public transportation, there is plane service to Louisville and to Evansville. Contact the Guest Master for more details.

History: St. Meinrad Archabbey was founded in 1854 by monks of Einsiedeln Abbey, Switzerland. Originally the monks ministered among the German Catholic population, later expanding their efforts to work among the Indians and to education. A college and seminary are located at the abbey today.

Description: The abbey is picturesquely perched above the banks of the nearby river. Guests are welcome to join the monks in worship in the abbey church, which is large, historic, and newly renovated.

Special Note: For information about group retreats contact Br. Maurus Zoeller, O.S.B., at (800) 581-6905.

Mississippi Abbey

8400 Abbey Hill
Dubuque, Iowa 52003

Telephone: (319) 582-2595. (Call between 9:00 A.M. and 11:30 A.M.)

Order: Cistercian (Trappistine) nuns (Roman Catholic).

Accommodations: Eleven women in single and twin rooms in three houses, all with shared bath.

Meals: The nuns provide food for all the retreat houses, and guests cook their own meals.

Charges: Freewill offering accepted.

Write or telephone: The Guest Secretary.

Directions: If driving from Dubuque, take Locust Street (Route 151/61 south) to Highway 52. Turn left (south) onto Highway 52 and travel for about five or six miles. The abbey sign will be on the right, directing a left turn onto Hilkens Road. It is about a twenty-minute drive from Dubuque.

For those using public transportation, there are plane and bus services to Dubuque.

History: The history of the Cistercian nuns closely parallels that of the monks of the same order. The Cistercians are an eleventh-century reform of the Benedictine order. A further reform was initiated at the abbey of La Trappe, France, in 1664. Trappistine nuns (as they are often called) from Ireland and England opened an American foundation in Wrentham, Massachusetts, and in 1964 twelve nuns from Wrentham opened Mississippi Abbey.

Description: Mississippi Abbey has about 580 acres of property, including bluffs, woods, and creeks that guests are free to explore. The nuns run a farm on which they produce their own food, and their main industry is the manufacture and sale of Trappistine Creamy Caramels.

Points of Interest: Marquette explored this area, and Dubuque was the first Roman Catholic archdiocese west of the Mississippi River. The Stone House (one of the guest houses) is an old country farmhouse dating from the mid-nineteenth century.

Special Note: The Stone House is open from March to November 1. The retreat house and cabin are open from the third Monday of January until December. Retreats are usually booked two months in advance, although there are sometimes last-minute cancellations. Reservations are limited during the months of November and December because of the busy schedule at the candy house at that time.

New Melleray Abbey

6500 Melleray Circle
Peosta, Iowa 52068

Telephone: (319) 588-2319. (Best times to call: 9:30 A.M. to 11:30 A.M., 2:00 P.M. to 5:00 P.M., or 6:15 P.M. to 7:15 P.M.)

Facsimile: (319) 588-4117.

Order: Cistercian (Trappist) monks (Roman Catholic).

Accommodations: Twenty-five guests in the monastery in single rooms, each with private bath.

Meals: Three meals daily.

Charges: Suggested donation of $30 per person per day for room and meals.

Write, telephone, or fax: The Guest Master.

Directions: For those driving, the abbey is twelve miles south of Dubuque on Highway 151.

For visitors using public transportation, there are both air and Greyhound bus services to Dubuque. Please contact the Guest Master for further directions.

History: The namesake of New Melleray Abbey is Mount Melleray Abbey in Ireland. In 1849, Cistercian monks from Mount Melleray arrived in Iowa and founded this community.

Description: Enclosing a quadrangle, the monastery was built following a traditional monastic floor plan. Of particular note here is the abbey church. Built in 1868 as a multistory wing of the monastery, it was gutted in 1976. The upper floors were removed and the plaster stripped from the walls. The results are surprising and successful: a lofty abbey church of simple beauty and solid materials—exposed stone walls and wooden rafters. Both church and monastery are surrounded by pine forests. Beyond are cultivated fields where the monks farm.

Special Note: Guests are invited to New Melleray Abbey as a place of spiritual retreat.

St. Benedict's Abbey Guest House
1020 North 2nd Street
Atchison, Kansas 66002

Telephone: (913) 367-7853.

Facsimile: (913) 367-6230.

Order: Benedictine monks (Roman Catholic).

Accommodations: Twelve guests in twin-bedded rooms, each with private bath.

Meals: Three meals daily.

Charges: $40 per person per day for room and meals.

Write, telephone, or fax: Fr. Blaine Schultz, O.S.B., Guest Master.

Directions: If you are driving from Kansas City, Missouri, or KCI (Kansas City International Airport), the fastest route to Atchison is the following: Get on I-29 going north. As you pass Platte City, take Exit 20, which lists Weston, Atchison, Leavenworth, and Highway 273. Follow 273 until it joins 45 at a red blinking light. Turn right. You will pass through the outskirts of Weston.

After about fifteen miles, you will see a small lake on the left. Prepare to turn left off 45 onto Highway 59, heading west. After four miles you will cross a bridge over the Missouri River and arrive in Atchison. At the foot of the bridge, turn right and cross the railroad tracks. At the first red light, turn right for two blocks, then turn left onto 2nd Street. Go eight blocks and you will see the twin-towered church of St. Benedict's parish. Proceed one more block north, then turn right at the sign on the right saying "Benedictine College." The new Student Activity Center is straight ahead of you. Follow the winding road up the hill to the abbey, abbey church, and guest-house complex on your left. A curving parking lot is in front of the guest house. Look for the double glass-door entrance. Inside are the telephone operator and information desk.

There is no public transportation.

History: Monks arrived in Atchison in 1857, just two years after the former Indian Territory of Kansas was opened to settlers and four years before Kansas was admitted to the Union as a state. Education has always been a primary mission here. St. Benedict's College (for men) and Mount St. Scholastica College (for women) combined in recent years to form the coeducational Benedictine College, which today has an enrollment of 750 students. The seventy-five monks of St. Benedict's Abbey teach, administer parishes, and are engaged in missionary work in Brazil.

Description: The abbey and its guest house stand on a bluff high above the Missouri River. Here you'll find buildings with a wide variety of architectural styles. For example, the monastery, built in 1929, is a handsome English Tudor Revival design. In 1957, a century after the monks' arrival, the present abbey church was built. Its modern style is the work of architect Barry Byrne, a student of Frank Lloyd Wright. Inside the limestone edifice visitors will be impressed with the 270-foot-long nave, the 610-square-foot fresco, the outstanding organ (with nearly 2,000 pipes) and the crypt below with its chapels, shrines, and thirty-one altars dedicated to favorite saints.

Points of Interest: Atchison has many late-nineteenth-century Victorian-style houses, churches, and public buildings. Just eight blocks from the abbey is the birthplace of aviatrix Amelia Earhart. Drop by the Santa Fe Depot Visitors Center (200 South 10th) for a map of the city's historic walking and driving tour.

Gethsemani Abbey
Trappist, Kentucky 40051

Telephone: (502) 549-4133.

Order: Cistercian (Trappist) monks (Roman Catholic).

Accommodations: Thirty-one guests in single rooms in the guest house, each with private bath. The first and third weeks of the month are reserved for women.

Meals: Three meals daily.

Charges: Freewill donations accepted.

Write or telephone: Grace.

Directions: Take Route 31E south from Bardtown, Kentucky, then turn left on Route 247.

There is no public transportation to the abbey.

History: The Cistercians are a reform of the Benedictine order dating to the eleventh century. In the seventeenth century a further reform was led by the French Abbot de Rance of La Grande Trappe Abbey. These Cistercians of the Strict Observance have since been popularly known as Trappists. A group of Trappist monks journeyed from France and settled in Kentucky in 1848.

Description: The abbey has an extensive property on which the monks farm and tend to other work such as the production of cheese and fruitcake. Guests are welcome to walk in the gardens or the woodlands and to join the monks for worship in the large and historic abbey church.

Points of Interest: Gethsemani Abbey was the home of Thomas Merton.

Special Note: The weekend retreat is from Friday afternoon to Sunday afternoon (or Monday morning). The midweek retreat is from Monday morning to Friday morning. The first and third weeks of each month are reserved for women. These weeks start on Mondays.

Brochures and further information are available.

St. Joseph Abbey
St. Benedict, Louisiana 70457

Telephone: (504) 892-1800. (Best time to call: 9:00 A.M. to 5:00 P.M.)

Facsimile: (504) 867-2270.

Order: Benedictine monks (Roman Catholic).

Accommodations: Nine men in the monastery in single rooms, each with private bath.

Meals: Three meals daily.

Charges: $10 for room and $20 for meals per person per day.

Write, telephone, or fax: The Guest Master.

Directions: If driving from points east or west, take I-12 to US 190 north.

If driving from points north or south (New Orleans is one hour south), take US 190 to Covington. In Covington, take LA 437 (Lee Road) east, then make a left onto River Road. The abbey will be on your right.

For those using public transportation, there is Greyhound bus service to Covington. Please contact the Guest Master for further directions.

History: St. Joseph Abbey was founded in 1890 by monks from St. Meinrad Archabbey, Indiana. From the beginning their principal work has been their seminary. More recently their work has expanded to include retreats, an Elderhostel program, a summer camp for boys and girls, and "Pennies for Bread and the Abbey," a program that supplies abbey-baked bread to the poor and needy in the area. St. Joseph is home to about fifty monks today.

Description: Bordered by the Bogue-Falaya River, the abbey's 1,200 acres combine cultivated areas and forests of pine and hardwoods. The abbey church is a massive classical revival building. The interior walls of the church and the monastic dining hall are covered with stunning murals, painted over the course of a decade by the Belgian artist/monk Dom Gregory de Wit.

Points of Interest: The abbey is just seven miles north of the beautiful Lake Pontchartrain.

Special Note: In addition to accommodating men in the monastery, the abbey opens its doors to men and women at the Abbey Christian Life Center. Built in 1965, the Center offers modest but comfortable rooms with private baths for up to forty-one persons.

Bay View Villa

187 Bay View Road
Saco, Maine 04072

Telephone: (207) 283-3636 or 286-8762. (Best time to call:
9:00 A.M. to 5:00 P.M.)

Facsimile: (207) 282-7376.

Order: Servants of the Immaculate Heart of Mary (Roman Catholic).

Accommodations: Forty-two guests in thirty-three rooms in the
convent, some with private bath.

Meals: Continental breakfast only. Dinner and supper on request.

Charges: Rates vary according to season. Single rooms range from
$25 in winter to $35 in summer. Double room with bath varies
from $45 in winter to $75 in summer. Double rooms without bath
range from $35 in winter to $60 in summer. Rates are per room
and include continental breakfast.

Write, telephone, or fax: The Director.

Directions: If driving from Maine Turnpike north (I-95), take Exit 5 to Saco/Old Orchard Beach. After you pay toll, continue straight (about three miles).

> Do not turn off on Industrial Park Road (Exit 1).
> Do not take Saco/Route 1 (2A).
> Do not take Scarborough (Exit 2B).

Just keep going straight until the road merges with Route 5. You are on Route 5 South. At a fork in the road you will leave Route 5 South, which turns left. Go straight on the narrower road—Temple Avenue. At the blinking traffic light, turn right onto Route 9 West (West Grand-Seaside Avenue) for one-and-one-half miles. Look for a large four-story gray building on the left.

> There is no public transportation.

History: The Servants of the Immaculate Heart of Mary have their roots in Quebec. It was there that Marie Josephte Fitzbach (known as Mother Mary) founded the Good Shepherd Congregation. In 1882 the American branch took root in New England, ministering to French Canadian immigrants. The sisters have opened their home—Bay View Villa—to visitors and guests for nearly a half century.

Description: The rooms at Bay View Villa are bright and airy and either front the ocean, have an ocean view, or offer a wooded view. The dining room has a picture window overlooking the Atlantic Ocean. Other amenities include a lounging room, an auditorium, a chapel, and screened-in porches facing the ocean, woods, and spacious lawns. The distinctive and charming mansard-roofed villa sits on the seven-mile beach of Saco Bay. A state park is just 1,000 feet away.

Points of Interest: Bay View Villa is minutes from Maine's beaches, parks, shopping centers, and theaters.

Special Note: As one sister put it, "People love it here—heaven on earth," inviting readers to "come and see."

All Saints Convent

Post Office Box 3127
Catonsville, Maryland 21228

Telephone: (410) 747-4104. (Call between 10:00 A.M. and noon, between 2:00 P.M. and 3:00 P.M., or between 3:30 P.M. and 4:45 P.M.)

Order: All Saints Sisters of the Poor (Episcopal).

Accommodations: Nine women in the convent in single rooms, all with shared bath.

Meals: Three meals daily.

Charges: Freewill offering.

Write or telephone: The Guest Mistress.

Directions: If driving, take I-95 and exit at Catonsville (Exit 47) to Rolling Road (Route 166). When Rolling Road meets Hilton Avenue, make a very sharp left. The convent is at the end of Hilton Avenue.

If using public transportation, take a plane to Baltimore-Washington International Airport or a train to BWI Airport Rail Station. Arrange ahead for possible pickup on arrival.

History: Founded in London in 1851, the sisters were named for the parish they served: All Saints, Margaret Street. In 1872 a group was sent to Baltimore to work among the city's poor, and in 1917 a gift was made of the Catonsville property. For more than a century the sisters have carried on a number of charitable projects, including schools, a summer day camp for inner-city children, a home for elderly women, care for the terminally ill, and retreat work. The All Saints Scriptorium is widely known, and greeting cards are sold at the Convent Card Shop and by mail order.

Description: The beautiful stone Gothic Revival chapel and convent are set on eighty-eight acres of natural woodlands, all of which is surrounded by state park lands.

Points of Interest: The convent is contiguous with Patapsco Valley State Park where there are numerous trails for walks and hikes.

Special Note: St. Gabriel's Retreat House on the convent grounds offers retreats for groups of up to twenty-five persons. Contact the Guest Mistress for brochures and further information on individual retreats in the convent and group retreats at St. Gabriel's.

Annunciation Monastery

Post Office Box 21238
Catonsville, Maryland 21228

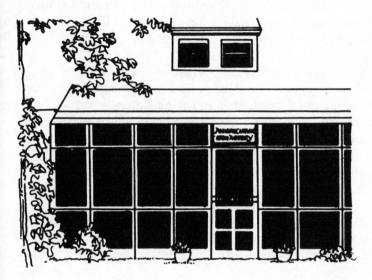

Telephone: (410) 747-6140. (Call between 9:30 A.M. and 7:00 P.M.)

Order: All Saints Sisters of the Poor (Episcopal).

Accommodations: Six men in the monastery, each with single room and all with shared bath.

Meals: Three meals daily.

Charges: Freewill offering.

Write or telephone: The Resident Chaplain.

Directions: If driving, take I-95 and exit at Catonsville (Exit 47) to Rolling Road (Route 166). When Rolling Road meets Hilton Avenue, make a very sharp left. The monastery and All Saints Convent are at the end of Hilton Avenue.

If using public transportation, take a plane to Baltimore-Washington International Airport or a train to BWI Airport Rail Station. Arrangements can be made for pickup on arrival.

Description: Annunciation Monastery is a ministry of the All Saints Sisters of the Poor. It is a wood-frame house on the property of the sisters' motherhouse. The monastery is surrounded by nearly ninety wooded and landscaped acres and, beyond that, state park lands.

Points of Interest: Patapsco Valley State Park, contiguous with the All Saints property, offers opportunities for walks and hikes.

Special Note: The Resident Chaplain may be contacted for a brochure, map, and more information. There is a daily Eucharist at the convent, and monastic hours at the convent and the monastery.

Emery House

Emery Lane
West Newbury, Massachusetts 01985

Telephone: (508) 462-7940.

Facsimile: (508) 462-0285.

Order: Society of St. John the Evangelist (Episcopal).

Accommodations: Up to twelve guests in the guest house and in hermitages, some with private baths.

Meals: Three meals daily.

Charges: $55 per person per day for room and meals.

Write, telephone, or fax: The Guest Master.

Directions: If driving, take I-95 to Route 113; continue west for 1¼ miles to Emery Lane on your right.

For those using public transportation, there are Greyhound and C & J Trailways bus services to Newburyport.

History: This farmhouse, which dates back to the eighteenth century, was given to the Society of St. John the Evangelist (Cowley Fathers) in 1952. In recent years the house had been used as a retreat, and in 1987 the Chapel of the Transfiguration and a cluster of hermitages were added.

Description: Emery House is situated on more than one hundred acres of field and woodland bordered by the Merrimack and Artichoke rivers.

Points of Interest: About a half mile down the road from the house is a four-hundred-acre state park with trail. The historic seaport city of Newburyport is at the mouth of the Merrimack River. Newburyport has become a model for historic preservation projects.

Special Note: Group retreats are given at Emery House on occasion; a calendar may be obtained from the Guest Master. Reservations must be made in writing, and a nonrefundable, nontransferable deposit of $55 is necessary to secure a reservation.

Glastonbury Abbey

16 Hull Street
Hingham, Massachusetts 02043

Telephone: (617) 749-2155. (Best time to call: Monday through Friday 8:00 A.M. to 2:00 P.M.)

Order: Benedictine monks (Roman Catholic).

Accommodations: Twenty-nine guests in two guest houses. There are twenty-two rooms (single and twin), some of which have private baths.

Meals: Three meals daily.

Charges: Suggested minimum offering of $45 to $50 per night for room and meals.

Write or telephone: The Retreat Secretary.

Directions: By car from Boston, take I-93 south (Southeast Expressway) to Route 3 south (to Cape Cod) to Exit 14, "Route 228, Rockland-Hingham." Follow Route 228 north (Main Street, Hingham) about seven miles to the abbey.

Driving I-95 from Rhode Island, Connecticut, and New York, take I-93 north (toward Boston). Follow I-93 north to Route 3 south (to Cape Cod), getting off Route 3 at Exit 14, "Route 228, Rockland-Hingham." Take Route 228 north (Main Street, Hingham) for about seven miles to the abbey.

If driving from the Massachusetts Turnpike (I-90), get off the pike at I-95 and go south. This road becomes I-93 north—be sure to stay on this road. Follow I-93 to Route 3 south (to Cape Cod), getting off Route 3 at Exit 14 (as above).

By public transportation from Boston, take the "T" (subway) Red Line Braintree train to Quincy Center Station. Then take the "220 Hingham" bus to the last stop (Station Street). Call the abbey for pickup if prior arrangement has been made. An alternate means of public transportation from Boston is the Plymouth and Brockton Busline, which leaves from South Station. Take a "Scituate" bus. Buy a "Hingham-Main Street" ticket. Ask to be let off at the monastery (last stop in Hingham). This is a very limited bus service, with no runs whatsoever on the weekend.

History: At the invitation of the late Cardinal Cushing, monks from Benet Lake, Wisconsin, founded this monastery in 1954. It was the first Benedictine monastery in the Commonwealth of Massachusetts.

Description: The abbey is located on sixty wooded acres less than two miles from the Atlantic Ocean. The guest houses, Stonecrest and Whitting Houses, are informal and comfortable homes, non-institutional in character.

Points of Interest: Hingham is a historic town (founded in 1635) just sixteen miles south of Boston. The Old Ship Church (1681) in Hingham is the last remaining Puritan meetinghouse in America.

Special Note: In addition to extending hospitality to individual guests, the abbey has a full schedule of group retreats. A calendar and further information are available from the abbey's Guest Master.

Monastery of St. Mary and St. John

980 Memorial Drive
Cambridge, Massachusetts 02138

Telephone: (617) 547-7330 or (617) 876-3037.

Order: Society of St. John the Evangelist (Episcopal).

Accommodations: Sixteen guests in single rooms in the guest house. Each room has its own sink; toilets and showers are nearby.

Meals: Three meals daily.

Charges: Suggested donation of $50 per person per day for room and meals (see Special Note below).

Write or telephone: The Guest Master.

Directions: If driving from Route 128, take Route 2 east. Make a left onto Memorial Drive. The monastery will be on the left. Contact the Guest Master for parking directions.

If using public transportation, take the "T" (subway) Red Line to Harvard Square. Walk down J. F. Kennedy Street to Memorial Drive. Make a right onto Memorial Drive.

History: The Society of St. John the Evangelist, the oldest monastic community in the Anglican communion, was founded by the Reverend Richard Meux Benson in 1866. The society was begun near Oxford, England, in the village of Cowley—St. John. For that reason, members of the society in the past had been popularly called the "Cowley Fathers." In 1870 the fathers came to Boston, Massachusetts, later settling their American motherhouse across the Charles River in Cambridge.

Description: The monastery was designed by architect Ralph Adams Cram, and the granite church is considered by many to be one of his masterpieces. The guest house, church, and monastery are all attached and occupy a small plot of land. Guests are free to walk along the Charles River across the road and to enjoy the wider expanse and fresh air.

Points of Interest: The monastery is virtually on the doorstep of Harvard University, and the "T" (subway) in Harvard Square provides easy access to the sights of Boston and its environs.

Special Note: The guest house is closed on Mondays until 5:00 P.M. and during the months of July and August, and for other brief periods. Reservations must be made in writing, and a nonrefundable deposit of $50 is necessary to secure a reservation. If it is not possible for a guest to give the suggested donation, arrangements can be made with the Guest Master. Group retreats are given at the monastery, and a brochure, calendar, and other information are available from the Guest Master.

St. Benedict Abbey

252 Still River Road
Still River, Massachusetts 01467

Telephone: (508) 456-3221.

Order: Benedictine monks (Roman Catholic).

Accommodations: Sixty guests (in the guest house) in single and twin-bedded rooms, some with private baths.

Meals: Three meals daily.

Charges: $25 per person per day for room and meals.

Write or telephone: The Guest Master.

Directions: If driving from the Boston area, take Route 2 west to Route 110/111 toward the town of Harvard. From the south, west, or north, take Route 495 to Route 117 west to Route 110 (Still River Road).

If using public transportation, take commuter rail from Boston to Ayer, Massachusetts. Arrange in advance with the Guest Master for pickup on arrival or take a taxi.

Description: The abbey is situated on seventy acres of woodland and fields overlooking Mount Wachusett and the Nashoba Valley. Several colonial homes form the abbey. The monks' house dates to 1683 and has been decorated and furnished with paintings and chairs of the period. The chapel is a former carriage shed in which the traditional Gregorian plainchant is sung. The 250-year-old guest house is available to individual guests, families, and groups. In addition to bedrooms, it has several living rooms, a conference room, a library, and a small chapel.

Points of Interest: Historic Lexington and Concord are near the abbey, as is Fruitlands Museum. Fruitlands is the remains of an eighteenth-century Utopian Transcendental community, which, like the abbey, overlooks the valley.

St. Joseph's Abbey
Spencer, Massachusetts 01562

Telephone: (508) 885-8710. (Call between 9:00 A.M. and 11:00 A.M., and between 1:30 P.M. and 5:00 P.M.)

Order: Cistercian (Trappist) monks (Roman Catholic).

Accommodations: Eleven men in the retreat house, each in single room with private bath.

Meals: Three meals daily.

Charges: Freewill offerings, but the average minimum has been about $25 to $30 per day for room and meals.

Write or telephone: The Guest Master.

Directions: If driving, take the Massachusetts Turnpike (I-90) to Exit 10 (Auburn). Then go onto Route 12 and Route 20 west for three miles. Go right onto Route 56 to Leicester (eight miles), then left on Route 9 to Spencer (nine miles). From Route 9 make a right onto Route 31 to the abbey (five miles).

If flying, take a flight to Worcester Airport and then a taxi to the abbey.

History: This community is the descendant of the Abbey of Our Lady of the Valley, Cumberland, Rhode Island. After the Rhode Island abbey burned in 1950, the monks resettled in Spencer. The new abbey, with its exterior of fieldstones hauled from the surrounding farmlands, was built by the monks in 1952–1953 under the supervision of an architect and contractor. Today the monks support themselves in part through the production and sale of Trappist Preserves. The Holy Rood Guild at the abbey designs and sells liturgical vestments.

Description: The abbey property includes nearly two thousand acres of woodland and cultivated fields. The retreat house is attached to the monastery and abbey church, where guests are encouraged to join the monks at services.

Special Note: A weekend retreat at the Abbey Retreat House begins on Friday afternoon and ends on Sunday after lunch. The mid-week retreat extends from Monday afternoon until Friday morning. One conference is given each day. Reservations must be made in advance. In addition to the Abbey Retreat House, there are two guest houses within a mile that, though independent of the abbey, are closely affiliated with it. Mary House is a place of solitude and retreat. Brunelle House is a lodge for informal stays. The abbey's Guest Master will provide literature and information on the Abbey Retreat House, Mary House, and Brunelle House.

St. Margaret's Convent

17 Highland Park Street
Roxbury, Massachusetts 02119

Telephone: (617) 445-3895.

Order: Society of St. Margaret (Episcopal).

Accommodations: Fourteen guests in the convent, most in single rooms and most with shared baths. In addition, the Carriage House has a spacious second-floor apartment with room to house four guests in two bedrooms. The apartment has a small kitchen where light meals may be prepared.

Meals: Three meals daily are shared with the sisters.

Charges: $40 per person per night for room and meals.

Write or telephone: The Guest Sister.

Directions: Please contact the Guest Sister for directions by car.

If using public transportation, take the Boston "T" (M.B.T.A. subway) Orange Line to Roxbury Crossing Station.

It is about a ten-minute walk up the hill to the convent or you may prefer to call for a cab.

History: The Society of St. Margaret was founded in England in 1855 by John Mason Neale (priest, hymnologist, and author). In 1873 the Society came to Boston to supervise nurses at the Children's Hospital and later extended its ministry to other areas. The Roxbury property, the former home of the great abolitionist William Lloyd Garrison, was acquired in 1907. The Society administered St. Monica's Home here for many years. In 1989 it was decided to move the Society's American motherhouse from Louisburg Square on Beacon Hill to the Fort Hill, Roxbury, property.

Description: St. Margaret's Convent is on a rocky hill of almost five acres just three miles from downtown Boston. There has been much new construction and renovation of the former St. Monica's Home to create a modern, light-filled, cheerful, and energy-efficient facility. While the convent is in a convenient location, it is somewhat removed from urban distractions and diversions.

Points of Interest: Boston, a very historic and cultured city, is easily accessible from the convent.

Special Note: In addition to welcoming individual guests, the convent welcomes groups at the DeBlois Conference Center, located on its property. The Center can accommodate up to fifty persons for meetings, retreats, and conferences. Contact the Guest Sister for more information.

St. Marina's Guest House and Bertram Conference Center

Harden Hill Road
Duxbury, Massachusetts

Telephone: (617) 445-8961.

Order: Society of St. Margaret (Episcopal).

Accommodations: In St. Marina's Guest House, eight guests, most in single rooms, all with shared baths.

In Bertram Conference Center, twenty guests in ten rooms with bunk beds, all with shared bath.

Meals: Please contact the Guest Sister regarding meals.

Charges: At St. Marina' Guest House there is a daily charge of $40. At the Bertram Conference Center the charge is $25 per person per day.

Write or telephone: St. Marina's Guest Sister, c/o St. Margaret's Convent, 17 Highland Park Street, Boston, MA 02119-1436
Telephone: (617) 445-8961.

Directions: If driving from the Boston area, take the Southeast Expressway (Route 3) south to Exit 10. Follow Route 3A north about one mile to a blinking light. Turn right and follow the signs to South Duxbury. At the flagpole, cross over, leaving the liquor store on your right and the Exxon station on your left. You will be on Washington Street. After about one-quarter mile, Harden Hill Road will be on your right. Turn right and Bertram Conference Center is the first building on your right. St. Marina's Guest House is the last building on the left side of the road.

For those using public transportation from Boston, the Plymouth and Brockton Busline has service to its terminal in Plymouth. Arrange in advance with the Guest Sister for a ride to the guest house.

History: The town of Duxbury was founded by settlers from Plymouth, perhaps as early as 1628. Prior to the American Revolution it was mainly a farming community. Following the Revolution, the fishing and shipbuilding industries prospered during the Golden Age of Shipbuilding in the period between the War of 1812 and the Civil War. The Society acquired this site in 1904 to be used as a refuge from hot Boston summers.

Description: Guests may enjoy beautiful views of Duxbury Bay from the front porch of the guest house as well as from most guest-room windows. Both the guest house and the chapel are charming shingle-style buildings; the enchanting guest cabin nearest the bay was once used in shipbuilding. The property has its own private beach.

Points of Interest: Duxbury is a very old and quaint residential town. It is a twenty-minute car ride from Duxbury to Plymouth. There Plymouth Rock, Mayflower II, and the reconstructed Plimouth Plantation may be visited. Beyond Plymouth is Cape Cod, easily accessible on a day trip.

Special Note: St. Marina's Guest House welcomes individual guests between June and September. However, groups may use Bertram Lodge year-round. Please contact the Guest Sister for more information.

St. Scholastica Priory

271 North Main Street
Post Office Box 606
Petersham, Massachusetts 01366-0606

Telephone: (508) 724-3213 and (508) 724-3216.

Facsimile: (508) 724-3574.

Order: Benedictine nuns (Roman Catholic).

Accommodations: Eighteen guests in twelve single and three double rooms, all with shared baths.

Meals: Three meals daily. The main meal is at midday.

Charges: Freewill.

Write, telephone, or fax: The Guest Mistress.

Directions: By car from Boston, take Route 2 west to Athol/Petersham Exit 17 (Route 32). Make a right turn at the bottom of the ramp onto Route 32 south. The priory is on the right after the Harvard University Forest and before the Petersham Country Club.

For those using public transportation, there is bus service from Boston to Orange or Gardner, Massachusetts. One of the nuns can meet you if prior arrangement has been made.

History: St. Scholastica Priory is unique in that it has a close association with the Benedictine monks of St. Mary's Monastery, a daughter house of Pluscarden Abbey, Scotland. These are located on the same property in Petersham, separate monastic communities but sharing the liturgy in the common church and cooperating closely in other areas. In 1996 the new church was dedicated, a magnificent Romanesque structure. The nuns and the monks conduct the liturgy in a mixture of Latin Gregorian chant with some English, according to the post–Vatican II reforms. This is a contemplative monastery that supports itself by the operation of St. Bede's publications and contributions.

Description: The monastery is housed in a stone manor house. The guest house is in a wood and brick building, formerly the monks' monastery. Petersham is close to Massachusetts' scenic Pioneer Valley and the Five-College area of Amherst and Northampton.

Points of Interest: The priory is close to the immense (128 square miles) Quabbin Reservoir, where visitors may enjoy scenic drives as well as opportunities for hiking and fishing. The Harvard University Forest, across the street, also has marked trails and a nature museum.

Dormition of the Mother of God Orthodox Monastery

3389 Rives Eaton Road
Rives Junction, Michigan 49277

Telephone/facsimile: (517) 569-2873. (Best times to call: 10:00 A.M. to 4:00 P.M. and 8:00 P.M. to 9:00 P.M.)

Order: Nuns (Romanian Episcopate of the Orthodox Church in America).

Accommodations: Fourteen guests in seven twin-bedded rooms in the guest house, all with shared baths.

Meals: Three meals daily.

Charges: Donations.

Write, telephone, or fax: The monastery.

Directions: If driving from points east or west, take I-94 to Exit 138, Jackson/Lansing, Route 127 north. Follow the signs to Lansing. Exit at Berry Road/Rives Junction. Turn left on Berry Road. Pass the first red barn on the left and the Baptist Church on the right. Continue to the first stop sign and turn right on Rives Eaton Road. Pass the open field on the left and enter the monastery after the second barn.

For those using public transportation, there is air service to Lansing Airport (forty-five minutes away) and Detroit Metro Airport (ninety minutes away). There are rental cars available, or visitors may possibly be met with prior arrangement, depending on schedule of services, monastery activities, availability of a driver, and so forth. There is also Greyhound bus service to Jackson. Pickup at the bus station is provided if prior arrangements have been made.

History: The monastery was founded in 1987 by the Very Reverend Mother Benedicta, its first abbess, and two other nuns. Following the retirement of Mother Benedicta, the Very Reverend Mother Gabriella became abbess in 1992. Archimandrite Roman Braga serves the community as spiritual father. The self-supporting community of the monastery now has ten sisters and two monk-priests.

Description: The monastery is located on forty-nine acres of woodland with an array of wildlife, providing "a place for restoration and refreshment of mind, body, and soul. The quiet and tranquil atmosphere provides a place for spiritual guidance and growth." Here are a chapel, a century-old farmhouse, a guest house, and a large pavilion for outdoor celebrations. "A vegetable garden, a flower garden, an orchard, and a cemetery complete the rustic landscape of this blessed place." The nuns hope to build a traditional Byzantine-style church, a new guest house, and more expansive housing for the community. The concept of the new monastery buildings—architecturally and spiritually—is based on the tradition of Eastern monasticism.

Points of Interest: Eighty miles east of Rives Junction is historic Greenfield Village.

Special Note: The monastic community produces and sells prayer ropes, glass-beaded decorated eggs, hand-painted icons, ecclesiastical vestments and altar clothes, beeswax candles, incense and incense burners, and other religious articles. It also has its own publishing house, HDM Press. Its monastic journal, *The Burning Bush,* is published three times annually and is free upon request.

St. Augustine's House

3316 East Drahner Road
Post Office Box 125
Oxford, Michigan 48371

Telephone: (810) 628-5155 (office) and (810) 628-2604 (guest house).

Order: Congregation of the Servants of Christ/Benedictines (Lutheran).

Accommodations: Six men in single rooms in the guest house, all with shared bath. There are also limited accommodations for one or two women.

Meals: Three meals daily. Lighter fare on ordinary Wednesdays and Fridays.

Charges: Suggested donation of $20 to $25 per person per day for room and meals.

Write or telephone: The Prior.

Directions: From the south (Detroit), take I-75 north to Pontiac. Exit onto M24 (Exit 81). Continue north on M24 to Oxford and turn east (right) onto East Drahner Road. St. Augustine's House is two-and-one-half miles east on the north side of East Drahner Road. From the north (Flint, Lapeer), take M24 south and turn left onto East Drahner Road.

If using public transportation, take a plane to Detroit and then limousine service to Pontiac. There are bus and train services to Pontiac, and train service to Lapeer.

History: This, the only Lutheran monastery in the United States, was founded in 1958 by the Reverend Arthur Carl Kreinheder. Following World War II there was a rekindled interest in monastic life among Lutherans, especially in Europe. This community is an outgrowth of that movement. It follows the Rule of St. Benedict and is affiliated with the Evangelical Lutheran Church in America.

Description: The community owns forty acres of land in a pleasant rural setting. The retreat house, which stands on a hillside, has a beautiful view that in winter can extend for miles. The Chapel of the Visitation of the Blessed Virgin Mary was constructed from a rebuilt Quonset hut.

Special Note: Guest information and maps are available upon request.

St. Gregory's Abbey

56500 Abbey Road
Three Rivers, Michigan 49093

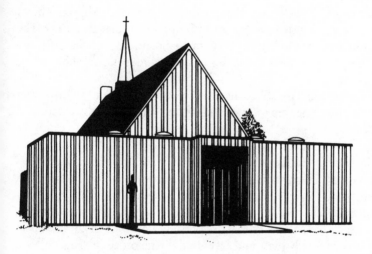

Telephone: (616) 244-5893. (Best times to call: 9:30 A.M. to 11:15 A.M. and 2:15 P.M. to 4:15 P.M., Eastern Time).

Order: Benedictine monks (Episcopal).

Accommodations: Eight men in single rooms in St. Anthony's Guest House. There are also accommodations for six women in single rooms in St. Denys Guest House. There are shared baths in each facility.

Meals: Three meals daily for men staying in the monastery. Women's meals are self-prepared in the guest house.

Charges: Freewill offerings accepted.

Write or telephone: The Guest Master.

Directions: If driving, take I-94 to Kalamazoo, then US 131 south. At Three Rivers, go right on Route 105, then right on Abbey Road (Route 103).

If using public transportation, take a plane, train, or bus to Kalamazoo, where a monk can meet you for transportation to the abbey.

History: The Anglican Benedictine monks of Nashdom Abbey, England, founded an American branch in Indiana in 1939. The monks moved to Three Rivers in 1946, and in 1969 St. Gregory's Priory was raised to the status of a fully independent abbey.

Description: The abbey, its church, monastery, guest house, and other buildings are in a parklike setting surrounded by woods and farmland.

Special Note: Reservations should be made as far in advance as is practical. The normal length of stay is from two days to one week. Weekend retreats for groups are scheduled from September through May. For an update, brochures, and further information, contact the Guest Master. The community invites all guests to participate in daily mass and sevenfold divine office (in English).

St. John's Abbey

Box 2015
Collegeville, Minnesota 56321-2015

Telephone: (320) 363-2573.

Facsimile: (320) 363-2504.

Order: Benedictine monks (Roman Catholic).

Accommodations: Twelve guests in the monastery in six twin-bedded rooms, each with its own bath.

Meals: Three meals daily.

Charges: Rooms are $25 per day, single occupancy, and $30 per day, double occupancy. Meals are $15 per person per day.

Write, telephone, or fax: The Guest Master.

Directions: If driving from Minneapolis (eighty miles away), take I-94 west to Exit 156.

For those using public transportation, Executive Express has a commuter service from the Minneapolis-St. Paul Airport directly to the abbey. (Call this company at 302-353-2226 in advance.)

History: Five pioneer/monks from St. Vincent's Archabbey (Pennsylvania) came to the Minnesota Territory in 1856, shortly after it was opened for settlement. Their primary missions were to work with the German immigrants in the area and to open a school for their children. Like many of their fellow pioneers, the first monks lived in log cabins. In time they made a permanent foundation in what is now called Collegeville, a beautiful wooded area between the Watab Creek and Lake Sagatagan. Today the monks number more than two-hundred members who teach, attend to the pastoral needs of Indians and others in the area, and pursue other endeavors. St. John's University was chartered by the territorial legislature in 1857. The campus is also the site of a prep school, the Liturgical Press, the Institute for Ecumenical and Cultural Research, KSJR-FM (founding station of Minnesota Public Radio), and the Hill Monastic Manuscript Library.

Description: St. John's has nearly 2,500 acres of land, of which 1,500 acres are wooded with twenty-four species of hardwoods. In 1988 the abbey embarked on a major environmental project: the restoration of 135 acres to their original native state. This includes a sixty-acre wetland, home to more than ninety species of water-fowl, songbirds, and fur-bearers. Further, in 1990 fifty acres were returned to their prairie state with more than one hundred species of grasses and wildflowers.

No description of St. John's would be complete without mentioning the Abbey and University Church designed by Marcel Breuer. A "Bell Banner" marks the church's entrance. Once inside, one becomes aware of the nave's monumental grandeur—225 feet in length, with a breadth of 180 feet.

Skete of the Resurrection of Christ

1201 Hathaway Lane
Minneapolis, Minnesota 55432

Telephone: (612) 574-1001.

Order: Monks (Synod of Bishops of the Russian Orthodox Church in Exile).

Accommodations: Two guests in single rooms in the skete, both with shared bath.

Meals: One complete meal served daily.

Charges: $50 per person per day for room and meal.

Write or telephone: Father Abbot.

Directions: If driving, take Highway 694 to Central Avenue North, then make a right to Hackman Street, and right again to Hathaway Lane.

If using public transportation, take the city bus #10M or #10N to Moore Lake.

History: A skete is a small community of monks, and in 1989 this small but growing community acquired its present home.

Description: With imagination and hard work the monks (and parishioners of the Church of the Resurrection of Christ) have transformed a suburban house into an inviting and functional monastery. At the heart of the skete is the Chapel of St. Seraphim. The icon screen in the chapel is old, having once stood in a cathedral. The traditional iconography, the chants in Old Church Slavonic and in English, and the incense and vestments all combine to create an intimate shrine with perhaps one of the finest expressions of Russian Orthodox liturgy outside Russia.

Points of Interest: The skete is just fifteen minutes from downtown Minneapolis and its parks, lakes, museums, and the IDS Center.

Special Note: Please call one month in advance for reservations.

Christ is risen from the dead,
trampling on death by death,
and on those in the tombs,
bestowing life.

Hymn for Easter
The Divine Liturgy of St. John Chrysostom

The Dwelling Place
HC-01 Box 126
Brooksville, Mississippi 39739

Telephone: (601) 738-5348. (Best times to call: Monday through Friday 9:00 A.M. to 4:30 P.M.)

Facsimile: (601) 738-5345.

Order: Franciscan sisters (Roman Catholic).

Accommodations: Eleven guests in seven rooms in the guest house or one of the hermitages, each with private bath.

Meals: Three meals daily.

Charges: $30 per person per day for room and $10 per person per day for meals.

Write, telephone, or fax: Sr. Clare Van Lent.

Directions: If driving, take Highway 45 to Brooksville. Two miles north of town, turn east at the "The Dwelling Place" sign at the three-way intersection. Drive exactly three miles. Look for the pine-lined lane and the white mailbox on the left.

There is no public transportation.

History: Our Lady of Portiuncula Chapel, dedicated in 1987, has a plaque at its entrance that tells the story of this special place:

> *In 1211, when the first men joined St. Francis of Assisi in his call to follow Christ, the Benedictine monks from Subiaco, Italy, gave Francis a little portion of land in the woods on which stood a tiny chapel named St. Mary of the Angels. The chapel later become known as St. Mary of the Portiuncula, Italian for* The Little Portion. *Several hermitages were built surrounding the chapel, and the Portiuncula became the birthplace of the Franciscan order.*
>
> *In 1985, Sr. Clare Van Lent, a Franciscan Sister, felt a call to ministry in Mississippi. The next year the Trappist monks, a reform group of Benedictines from New Melleray, Iowa, gave Sr. Clare a* Little Portion *of land, on which stands this tiny chapel, now named St. Mary of the Portiuncula.*

Description: The Dwelling Place includes three hermitages (Francis House, Clare House, and Maria House), Umbria Guest House, a dining room, library, and the chapel. The seventeen acres here are planted with 1,500 pine trees, providing beauty, shade, and a sanctuary for birds. Guests may wish to visit the pond with its shelter and footbridge.

Points of Interest: Brooksville is twenty-five miles from Columbus, Mississippi, and its many outstanding antebellum plantations. The area has a number of historic sites associated with the Civil War.

Special Note: The Dwelling Place publishes a newsletter complete with articles and information regarding its scheduled retreats. As Sr. Clare says, "We welcome 'pray-ers' anytime."

Assumption Abbey

Route 5, Box 1056
Ava, Missouri 65608-9142

Telephone: (417) 683-5110. (Best times to call: 9:30 A.M. to 11:30 A.M. and 2:30 P.M. to 5:00 P.M.)

Facsimile: (417) 683-5658.

Order: Cistercian (Trappist) monks (Roman Catholic).

Accommodations: Nine guests in single rooms in the monastery guest wing, with one bath for every two rooms.

Meals: Three meals daily.

Charges: Freewill offering.

Write, telephone, or fax: The Guest Master.

Directions: If driving on Route I-44, exit onto Route 5 just east of Springfield. Continue south on Route 5 to Route 14 east in Ava. Take a right onto Route 00 (gravel road). The abbey is on your left. Alternately, take Route 5 south, make a left onto Route N east, then left onto Route 00. The abbey will then be on your right.

If using public transportation, please contact the Guest Master regarding your best options.

History: In 1950 monks from New Melleray Abbey, Iowa, came to Missouri and founded Assumption Abbey. To support themselves during their first decade in their new home, the monks farmed and tended orchards and vineyards. In the 1960s, using sand and gravel from their land, they began to produce concrete blocks. This industry was successful for charitable and community needs, the blocks being used in the construction of a permanent monastery in 1970. Since the mid-1980s the monks have turned their efforts to baking fruitcakes, an endeavor that they find "suits our monastic rhythm well."

Description: Set amid crystal streams and rugged cliffs, the abbey is "an oasis of prayer, peace, and solitude."

The Sycamore Tree
Swan Lake, Montana 59911

Telephone: (406) 754-2429.

Order: Staffed by the Diocese of Helena (Roman Catholic).

Accommodations: Two guests in single rooms, one with private bath and one with shared bath. In the future there may be more hermitages to accommodate a larger number of guests.

Meals: As requested.

Charges: No established fee, but offerings are accepted as the Sycamore Tree is self-supporting.

Write or telephone: Fr. D.A. Okorn, Director.

Directions: "We are located 'off the beaten track'… If you would like more information, or would like to visit us, please write or call and we will give directions to the Sycamore Tree."

Description: The Sycamore Tree is located in the Swan Valley in the foothills of the Mission Mountains of Western Montana, a place of wooded panoramas, scenic beauty, and solitude. Aside from the hermitages, there is a chapel where guests are invited to join in daily services, as well as a well-stocked bookshop. The entire property consists of thirty acres, where you are invited to "stretch your body, mind, and spirit."

And, behold, there was a man named Zacchaeus, which was the chief among the publicans, and he was rich. And he sought to see Jesus who he was; and could not for the press, because he was little of stature. And he ran before, and climbed up into a sycamore tree to see him: for he was to pass that way. And when Jesus came to the place, he looked up, and saw him, and said unto him, Zacchhaeus, make haste, and come down; for to day I must abide at thy house. And he made haste, and came down, and received him joyfully.

—Luke 19:2–6

Christos the King Priory

St. Benedict Center
Post Office Box 528
Schuyler, Nebraska 68661

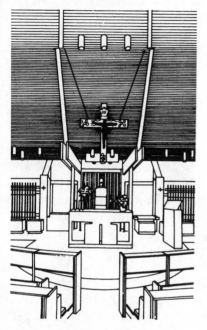

Telephone: (402) 352-8819.

Facsimile: (402) 352-8884.

Order: Benedictine monks (Roman Catholic).

Accommodations: Seventy-two guests in thirty-six twin-bedded rooms in St. Benedict Center, each with a private bath. In addition, there are accommodations for six men in single rooms in the monastic guest wing, each with private bath.

Meals: Three meals daily.

Charges: $40 per person per day for room and meals, single occupancy, and $35 per day for room and meals, double occupancy.

Write, telephone, or fax: The Administrator.

Directions: Schuyler is sixty miles west of Omaha at the junction of US Highway 30 and Nebraska Highway 15. St. Benedict Center and the priory are located four miles north of town from the intersection of Highways 15 and 30.

For those using public transportation, there is air service to Omaha (sixty-five miles west). Contact the Administrator for further directions.

History: The Benedictine Missionary Congregation of St. Ottilien was founded in Germany in the late nineteenth century. Fearing the worst for their abbey, a group of monks left Germany in the 1930s and settled in Nebraska, living more than forty years in an old frame farmhouse known as the Mission House, a development and education office for the congregation's missions in Africa, Asia, and South America. A new, strikingly modern monastery was completed in 1979, and in 1997 St. Benedict Center—an ecumenical retreat and conference center offering peace, tranquility, and hospitality to individuals and groups—opened.

Description: The priory is unique in that it is literally set into the natural landscape of the area, its roof and outer walls covered by a verdant carpet of grass. St. Benedict Center has a large chapel, meeting rooms, dining rooms, a solarium with library, a spacious lobby, and a gift shop filled with a large selection of Christian art, books, and items from mission countries. A permanent exhibit provides a history of this congregation, displaying artifacts from various countries. Guests may enjoy a park and lake for walks. Both the Center and the priory are surrounded by a broad expanse of farmland.

Points of Interest: Omaha is the home of the Strategic Aerospace Museum, the Western Heritage Museum, and the Joslyn Art Museum. Father Flanagan's Boys Town is just west of Omaha.

Wellspring Retreat House

Post Office Box 60818
701 Park Place
Boulder City, Nevada 89006

Telephone: (702) 293-4988.

Order: Sisters of Charity (Episcopal).

Accommodations: Forty guests in the retreat house in single, double, and twin rooms, as well as rooms for three and four guests. Some rooms have private baths.

Meals: Three meals daily.

Charges: $35 per person per night for room and breakfast only. $45 per person per day for room and three meals.

Write or telephone: Sr. Faith Mary, S.C.

Directions: If driving, take Business Route US 93 to Colorado Street. Continue through the park to Utah Street, then turn right and then left onto Park Place.

For those using public transportation, there are air, rail, and bus services to Las Vegas. Phone the retreat house in advance to arrange for pickup.

History: St. Vincent DePaul founded the Roman Catholic Sisters of Charity in seventeenth-century France. Inspired by his work, the Anglican Sisters of Charity were begun in Bristol, England, in 1869. Nearly a century later the Anglican sisters accepted an invitation to staff St. Jude's Ranch for abused and neglected children. Within a decade Wellspring was purchased. Originally a hospital to serve those building the Hoover Dam, Wellspring was placed on the National Register of Historic Places in 1987.

Description: Wellspring is an oasis in the desert surrounded by flowerbeds, pine trees, bushes, and cacti. There are fine views of the mountains and Lake Mead.

Points of Interest: The Hoover Dam, the Valley of First State Park, Red Rock Canyon, the Grand Canyon west rim, and Las Vegas are all close to Wellspring.

Special Note: In addition to welcoming individual guests, Wellspring also offers group retreats. Please contact the Guest Sister for information.

Epiphany Monastery

Post Office Box 60
Scobie Road
New Boston, New Hampshire 03070-0060

Telephone: (603) 487-3020. (Best times to call: 8:00 A.M. to 11:30 A.M. and 1:00 P.M. to 5:00 P.M.)

Facsimile: (603) 487-3700.

Order: Camaldolese monks (Roman Catholic).

Accommodations: Eleven guests in the guest house in single rooms, all with shared baths.

Meals: Three meals daily.

Charges: $30 per person per day.

Write, telephone, or fax: The Guest Master.

Directions: The monastery is located twenty miles west of Manchester, New Hampshire, and three-and-one-half miles from the center of the town of New Boston. If driving from Boston or Manchester, from I-293, take Route 101 to the Bedford exit, left lane, to Route 114 to Goffstown. Just past the large Exxon gas station, take a left onto Route 13 to New Boston (seven miles). At the stop sign and general store near the center of New Boston, turn right. After one block, turn right again onto Route 77. At the next fork, bear left to Route 136 west (to Francestown and Peterborough) and go for three miles. Turn left at Scobie Road, and go to the end of the paved road. Then turn right onto the unpaved continuation of Scobie Road. The first house on your right is Epiphany Monastery. Drive just past the house and its large white barn, taking a right into the parking area drive.

If driving from Brattleboro, Vermont, from I-91 north or south, take Brattleboro Exit 3 onto Route 9 east to Keene, New Hampshire. At Keene, take Route 101 east to Peterborough and then Route 202 north for two miles to Route 136 east through Francestown. After leaving Francestown, continue about four miles. Scobie Road enters deep woods on your right. At Scobie Pond, bear left and continue until you see the monastery sign. (If you miss the Scobie Road turnoff, you will soon come to the point where it rejoins Route 136. Take a right and follow directions given above.)

For those using public transportation, there are air and bus services to Manchester. Arrange in advance for pickup on arrival.

History: The Camaldolese are a branch of the Benedictine monastic family that dates back to the sixth century. St. Romuald, in eleventh-century Italy, reformed and revitalized both the communal and solitary aspects of monastic life, establishing the Camaldolese. Monks brought the Camaldolese Benedictine tradition to North America in 1958, establishing New Camaldoli Hermitage in the Santa Lucia Mountains at Big Sur on California's coast. It was in March 1993 that Epiphany Monastery was opened on the site of the former Hundred Acres Monastery in New Hampshire.

Description: The monastery is located in the beautiful rural woodlands of southern New Hampshire. The land is a tract of one hundred acres of forest. "Silent except for the wind blowing through the tall trees, it invites an awareness of God's presence." The wetlands and streams here attract a variety of wildlife. The monks live in a handsome eighteenth-century colonial house. Just steps away is a traditional New England barn that has been imaginatively converted into an attractive guest house, which includes a large library and a pleasant kitchen. Not far away is Scobie Pond, where guests may swim in summer or ice skate in winter.

Points of Interest: The Currier Gallery of Art is located in nearby Manchester. The southwestern corner of the state is often referred to as the "Currier and Ives corner of New Hampshire" because of its beautiful rolling hills, farmhouses, barns, country churches, cool summers, vibrant autumn foliage, and snow-covered winters. North of New Boston is the White Mountains Region with its Presidential Range including Mount Washington, the highest mountain in the northeast.

Convent of St. John Baptist and St. Marguerite's House

Post Office Box 240
82 West Main Street
Mendham, New Jersey 07945

Telephone: (201) 543-4641. (Best times to call: 10:00 A.M. to 12:00 noon and 1:00 P.M. to 5:00 P.M.)

Facsimile: (201) 543-0327.

Order: Community of St. John Baptist (Episcopal).

Accommodations: Six women in the convent, and twenty-six guests in St. Marguerite's House, each in a single room and all with shared baths.

Meals: Three meals daily.

Charges: $55 per person per day for room and meals.

Write, telephone, or fax: The Guest Mistress.

Directions: If driving from points north, take Route 80 or 78 to Route 287 south. Exit at Morristown Route 124 west. At Morristown Green, turn right on Washington Street (Route 24). Continue eight miles to Mendham. The convent is on the left.

From points south, take the Garden State Parkway or New Jersey Turnpike to Route 287 north. Exit at 22B. Follow 206 north to Chester. Turn right on Route 24 east and continue five miles to Mendham. The convent will be on the right.

If using public transportation, contact the Guest Mistress for directions.

History: The Community of St. John Baptist was begun in Windsor, England, in 1852 by the widow of an Anglican priest, Harriet Monsell, and the Reverend Thomas T. Carter. The purpose of the foundation was twofold: contemplative prayer and active service. It was in 1874 that the community came to the United States, first taking up residence in New York City and later moving to its more rural and peaceful surroundings in New Jersey. In 1908, St. Marguerite's House was built. At first a children's home, in 1960 it became a retreat house.

Description: St. Marguerite's House is a red brick re-creation of an English manor house. Numerous beautiful trees and shrubs surround St. Marguerite's, and beyond are ninety-three acres of wooded land, "which lends itself to prayer and meditation. Walking paths provide guests with the opportunity to experience God's beauty in nature." Just across the way is the Gothic Revival white-stuccoed convent. Guests are invited to join the sisters at their daily services in their chapel.

Points of Interest: There are a number of dairy farms in Mendham. Just eight miles down the road is Morristown National Historic Park. This was the main campsite of the American armies (and George Washington's headquarters) for two winters during the American Revolution.

Special Note: Generally, individual women guests are accommodated in the convent, and groups of men and/or women stay in St. Marguerite's House. Please contact the Guest Mistress regarding these accommodations and special programs.

St. Mary's Abbey Retreat Center

Delbarton
230 Mendham Road
Morristown, New Jersey 07960

Telephone: (201) 538-3231. (Best time to call: 8:00 A.M. to 5:00 P.M.)

Facsimile: (201) 538-7109.

Order: Benedictine monks (Roman Catholic).

Accommodations: Fifty guests in the guest house in thirty-four single and twin-bedded rooms, all with shared baths.

Meals: Three meals daily.

Charges: $50 per person per day for room and meals.

Write, telephone, or fax: The Guest Master.

Directions: If driving from New York City via the George Washington Bridge, take I-95 to I-80 west. Then take Route 287 south to Morristown Exit 35 (Route 124—old 24 Madison Avenue). Bear right at the end of the ramp onto Route 124 west (South Street). Proceed straight one mile to the Morristown Green. Travel three sides of the Green (do not take Route 202). Follow the sign for 510 west (Washington Street). This becomes Route 24 (Mendham Road). St. Mary's will be on the left—two-and-one-half miles from Morristown Green. Alternately, from New York City via the Lincoln Tunnel, take Route 3 west to US 46 west to I-80 west. Then proceed as directed above.

From points east or west, take I-80. From points north or south take Route 287. Take the Morristown Exit 35 and proceed as directed above.

If using public transportation, please contact the Guest Master for directions.

History: St. Mary's was founded not in Morristown, but in Newark, New Jersey, in 1857. The Morristown property—a former country estate—was bought in 1926. Thirty years later, in 1956, abbot and monks made the move to Morristown. True to Benedictine tradition, the monks teach at Delbarton—an excellent prep school—offer hospitality to retreatants, and minister to parishes here and in Brazil.

Description: "Delbarton" takes its name from the old estate that St. Mary's occupies today. The large granite mansion has a lovely Italian garden, complete with classical statuary. Farther up the hill is the abbey church, its red brick and starkly modern exterior contrasting sharply with the "Old Main" estate house. Surrounding all are 360 woodland acres with paths and splendid panoramic views of the countryside beyond.

Points of Interest: George Washington and the American armies camped for two winters in what is now Morristown National Historic Park.

Monastery of Christ in the Desert

Post Office Box 270
Abiquiu, New Mexico 87510

Telephone: (505) 470-4515.

Order: Benedictine monks (Roman Catholic).

Accommodations: Thirteen guests in the guest house in five single and four double rooms, all with shared baths.

Meals: Three meals daily.

Charges: There is no fixed charge, but $30 per person per day would cover the monastery's cost.

Write or telephone: The Guest Master.

Directions: The monastery is about seventy-five miles north of Santa Fe and about fifty-three miles south of Chama, New Mexico, off Route 84. About one mile south of the entrance sign for Echo Amphitheater or one mile north of Ghost Ranch Visitor's Center of the Carson National Forest (not to be confused with Ghost Ranch itself), the road for the monastery leaves Route 84 toward the west. This means that if one is coming from Santa Fe to the north, one turns to the left. Forest Service Road 151 (the name of the road to the monastery) is winding, steep, and narrow at some points. It has a dirt and clay surface and becomes very slippery when wet.

There is no public transportation to the monastery.

History: Three monks from Mount Saviour Monastery, New York, founded the Monastery of Christ in the Desert in 1964. The present monastic community began arriving in 1974 and is an independent priory of the Subiaco Congregation of Benedictines.

Description: The chapel, convent, and guest house, built of stone and adobe, are in a canyon 6,500 feet above sea level. This is surrounded by federal wilderness. The nearest neighbor is about fifteen miles away.

Points of Interest: Carson National Forest and Santa Fe National Forest are on either side of Abiquiu.

Special Note: It is essential to write to the Guest Master in advance for information on travel conditions, climate, and advice on what to bring.

Our Lady of Guadalupe Benedictine Abbey
Pecos, New Mexico 87552

Telephone: (505) 757-6415 or (505) 757-6600. (Call Monday to Friday 10:00 A.M. to noon and 1:15 P.M. to 3:00 P.M., and Saturday 10:00 A.M. to noon, Mountain Time.)

Order: Benedictine monks and oblate sisters in two communities (Roman Catholic).

Accommodations: Sixty guests in single and twin rooms in motel-style retreat units, each with private bath.

Meals: Three meals daily.

Charges: Please contact the reservations office for information regarding charges.

Write or telephone: Reservations Office.

Directions: If driving, take I-25 north to Glorieta and the Pecos exit, then turn right and continue seven miles to the town of Pecos. Then make a left turn and drive one mile to the monastery.

For those using public transportation, there is air service to Albuquerque, then a Shuttlejack bus to the Inn of Loretto in Santa Fe. There is bus service to Santa Fe and Amtrak train service to nearby Lamy. Arrange with the Reservations Office for pickup.

History: The monastery began in 1955 when the property was purchased by the Benedictines of Benet Lake, Wisconsin. In 1964 four monks from Benet Lake came to Pecos with the vision of establishing a charismatic Benedictine community. "As the community has developed, it has sought to deepen its monastic dimension, and although visible charismatic gifts are still to be enjoyed and shared, there is also a growing attention of the contemplative monastic tradition." In 1985 the community was joined to the Olivetan Congregation of the Benedictine Order.

Description: The 1,000-acre property is in the Sangre de Cristo ("Blood of Christ") Mountains at an altitude of 7,000 feet above sea level, located in the secluded Pecos River Valley.

Points of Interest: Santa Fe is twenty-five miles from the monastery. Guests may visit the many Indian reservations in the area.

Special Note: In addition to receiving individual guests, Our Lady of Guadalupe also offers group retreats. A $50 nonrefundable deposit is necessary to secure a reservation. Please contact the Reservations Office for more information and a retreat brochure.

Abbey of the Genesee

River Road
Piffard, New York 14533

Telephone: (716) 243-2220.

Order: Cistercian (Trappist) monks (Roman Catholic).

Accommodations: Sixteen guests in single rooms in Bethlehem House, all with shared bath. In addition, there are accommodations for up to thirty-one guests (men and women) in Bethany House and Cana House, all with shared bath.

Meals: Three meals daily in Bethlehem House. Guests may use the kitchen in Bethany and Cana Houses to prepare their own meals.

Charges: No fixed fee; freewill donations accepted.

Write or telephone: The Guest Master.

Directions: The Genesee Expressway, Route 390, provides easy access by car to Geneseo, New York. Traveling north or south along Route 390, take Exit 8 for Geneseo. At the Geneseo exit, proceed west on Route 20A. Turn right at Highway 63, north. In Piffard, turn right at River Road, north. A sign for the abbey will indicate the turn onto River Road.

If traveling west on the New York State Thruway, exit at Interchange 46, proceeding south on Route 390 to Exit 8, as previously outlined.

For those using public transportation, the nearest airport is Monroe County Airport in Rochester. There is also Amtrak service to Rochester, as well as Greyhound and Trailways bus services. There is Trailways bus service from Rochester to Geneseo. From there, taxi service, though expensive, is available. If necessary, the abbey can provide transportation from Geneseo if a previous arrangement is made.

History: Trappist monks from Gethsemani Abbey in Kentucky arrived in the Genesee Valley in 1951, having accepted the gift of a tract of land. The community originally lived in what is now Bethlehem Retreat House. The abbey church, built of stone and designed to express "an appropriate blend of modern and traditional elements," was completed in 1975.

Description: Across the road from Bethlehem House is Bethany, a stately nineteenth-century cobblestone house. Cana is a modern wood-frame dwelling just down the road. Each guest house is about a mile from the abbey church.

Points of Interest: Letchworth State Park is just south of the abbey.

Special Note: Brochures and guidelines on all three guest houses are available from the abbey's Guest Master.

Convent of St. Helena

134 East 28th Street
New York, New York 10016

Telephone: (212) 889-1124. (Best time to call: 6:00 P.M. to 7:30 P.M.)

Facsimile: (212) 779-4009.

Order: Order of St. Helena (Episcopal).

Accommodations: Two guests in the convent in one room with private bath.

Meals: Breakfast.

Charges: Suggested donation of $35 for bed and breakfast.

Write, telephone, or fax: Sr. Linda Julian, O.S.H.

Directions: Those driving should be aware that 28th Street is an eastbound one-way street; the convent is located between Lexington Avenue (southbound one-way) and Third Avenue (northbound one-way).

For those using public transportation, there is Carey Bus service from the airports to Grand Central Station. It is then a short Yellow Cab ride to the convent. If arriving by train at Grand Central Station or Penn Station, or by bus at the Port Authority Bus Terminal, it is best to take a Yellow Cab the short distance to the convent. Alternately, the subway stop nearest the convent is at Park Avenue and 28th Street (Lexington Avenue local—Green number 6). Buses numbers 101, 102, and 103 stop at 28th on Lexington Avenue (southbound) and at Third Avenue (northbound).

History: Begun in Kentucky in 1945, the Order of St. Helena came to New York State's Hudson River Valley in 1952. The order now has a presence in New York City, where the sisters are engaged in education and professional development, urban ministries, many kinds of social outreach, spiritual direction, diocesan life, and hospitality, including retreats, quiet days, pilgrimages abroad, and workshops.

Description: As in every house of the Order of St. Helena, the day at the Manhattan convent is centered on the celebration of the Eucharist and the office. This is a haven and a quiet oasis amid the noise, congestion, and distractions of midtown Manhattan.

Points of Interest: Visitors will find the United Nations, historic and beautiful churches, museums, libraries, and parks in close proximity to the convent.

Convent of St. Helena

Post Office Box 426
Vails Gate, New York 12584

Telephone: (914) 562-0592.

Order: Order of St. Helena (Episcopal).

Accommodations: Twenty-four guests in the guest house in eight single and eight twin rooms, all with shared baths.

Meals: Three meals daily.

Charges: Suggested donation of $50 per person per day for room and meals.

Write or telephone: The Guest Team.

Directions: If driving from east or west, take Interstate 84 to Exit 7S and then Route 300 south to its end at Five Corners in Vails Gate.

From north or south, take the New York State Thruway (I-87) to Exit 17. Turn right on 17K to the first light. Get in the left lane right away. Turn left on Route 300, follow to its end in Five Corners. From Five Corners bear left on Route 94. Go past the next light (Old Forge Hill Road) to the convent entrance just beyond on the right.

For those using public transportation, Short Line buses from New York City (Port Authority Terminal) to Vails Gate run every two hours. The ride is less than an hour and a half. Short Line also runs buses from Long Island and White Plains, and from Elmira and Binghamton, to Newburgh. There are Trailway buses from Albany. USAirways, Delta, and American Airlines fly to Stewart Field in Newburgh. Please arrange in advance with a member of the Guest Team to be met on arrival.

History: Founded in Kentucky in 1945, the Order of St. Helena moved its motherhouse in 1952 to "Forge Hill," a former estate on the outskirts of Newburgh, New York.

Description: The guest house, convent, and chapel are attached by a cloister. The newer buildings match the warm red-brick exterior of the former mansion, and all are set in a wooded area.

Points of Interest: The Hudson River, Bear Mountain, Washington's last headquarters, and other sights are close to the convent.

Special Note: The sisters welcome individual guests and also sponsor group retreats. Further information may be obtained from the Guest Team.

Holy Cross Monastery

Post Office Box 99
West Park, New York 12493

Telephone: (914) 384-6660.

Order: Order of the Holy Cross (Episcopal).

Accommodations: Up to thirty-nine guests in the guest house, each with a single room and all with shared bath.

Meals: Three meals daily.

Charges: $60 per day requested to cover the cost of room and meals.

Write or telephone: The Guest Master.

@ 1998

Directions: If driving, take the New York State Thruway (I-87) to Exit 18 (New Paltz), then take Route 299 east to Route 9W. Go north four miles; the entrance will be on your right.

If using public transportation, take the Metro North train from Grand Central Station in Manhattan to Poughkeepsie.

History: The Order of the Holy Cross has the distinction of being the oldest indigenous men's community in the Episcopal Church. The Reverend James Otis Sargent Huntington founded the order in New York City in 1884. After a couple of moves, he settled the Order's motherhouse at West Park in 1904.

Description: The monastery sits on the banks of the Hudson River in the Mid-Hudson Valley. The guest house is the original monastery and is connected with the church and newer monastery. Guests are welcome to join the community in worship and to dine with the monks in their refectory.

Points of Interest: West Park is situated directly across the Hudson River from Hyde Park, where one may visit the Vanderbilt Mansion as well as the Franklin D. Roosevelt home, library, and museum. West Point, historic Newburgh with Washington's last headquarters, and the Huguenot homes in New Paltz are also close by.

Special Note: Holy Cross Monastery welcomes individual guests and also sponsors group retreats. Contact the monastery for information.

Holy Myrrhbearers Monastery
144 Bert Washburn Road
Otego, New York 13825-9650

Telephone: (607) 432-3179.

Order: Nuns (Orthodox Church in America).

Accommodations: Five women or five men in the guest house in one single and two twin rooms, all with shared baths.

Meals: Three meals daily (strictly vegetarian).

Charges: "There is no set fee, but the sisters are grateful for contributions to help cover expenses, and for help with work from guests when possible."

Write or Telephone: The Guest Mistress.

Directions: Drivers will find that the monastery is close to I-88. Please call or write the monastery for a map.

For those using public transportation, the nearest airports are Binghamton, New York (one hour away) and Albany (two hours away). There is bus service to Oneonta, New York. Contact the monastery for further directions.

History: The beginnings of the Community of the Holy Myrrhbearers can be traced to 1977 when an Episcopal nun of thirteen years converted to the Orthodox Church. Later trained as an Orthodox nun at the Russian monastery in Bussy, France, she returned to the United States and was joined by other nuns. With the help of friends, the Otego property was purchased in 1983. Several neighboring parishes grouped to support the community in building an attractive chapel, providing the architectural plans and all labor.

In addition to attending liturgical services in their chapel, doing the usual household chores, and caring for the grounds and vegetable garden, the nuns work to support themselves as much as possible through a mail-order business offering greeting cards, bookmarks, certificates, and other items reproduced from calligraphy and artwork done by the sisters.

Description: The monastery has a 150-acre farm, which includes a beautiful pond. The old millhouse has been converted to the guest house.

Points of Interest: Historic Cooperstown, on Otsego Lake, is thirty minutes from the monastery.

House of the Redeemer

7 East 95th Street
New York, New York 10128

Telephone: (212) 289-0399.

Order: (An Episcopal Board of Trustees).

Accommodations: Fifteen guests in single and twin rooms, some with private baths.

Meals: Meals are provided for those participating in a group retreat of twelve or more. Refrigerator space is available for individual guests to store food.

Charges: $60 for a single, or $75 for a double room, per night. Ask about special group rates.

Write or telephone: Manager of Operations.

Directions: If driving from midtown Manhattan, head north on Madison Avenue and then left (west) on East 95th Street.

If using public transportation, take a Madison Avenue bus number M1, M2, M3, or M4 to 95th Street. By subway, take the Lexington Avenue Line #6.

History: The House of the Redeemer is the former Fabbri Mansion. Built between 1914 and 1916, it was the home of Edith Shepard (great-granddaughter of Commodore Cornelius Vanderbilt) and her husband Ernesto Fabbri. In 1949, Mrs. Fabbri converted her home into a retreat house, thereafter called the House of the Redeemer. It was designated a landmark by the Landmarks Preservation Commission in 1974. Staffed by the Episcopal Community of St. Mary until 1982, the house is under the steward-ship of an independent board of trustees.

Description: Designed by architect Grosvenor Atterbury, the house was built in the style of an Italian Renaissance palazzo or town house. The interior contains many exceptionally fine features, including the library with its woodwork from the fifteenth-century Ducal Palace in Urbino, Italy. Antiques, paintings, and furnishings all combine to make the House of the Redeemer an intact landmark.

Special Note: The House of the Redeemer welcomes clergy visiting New York City on official church business, as well as individuals who wish to participate in a group retreat. A schedule of retreats is available on request. Guests are expected to remain in the House for the duration of the retreat.

Little Portion Friary

Wayside House
48 Old Post Road
Post Office Box 399
Mt. Sinai, New York 11766

Telephone: (516) 473-0553. (Best time to call: 9:30 A.M. to 4:30 P.M.)

Order: Franciscan brothers (Episcopal).

Accommodations: Sixteen guests in three double and ten single rooms, all sharing three baths.

Meals: Three meals daily.

Charges: $50 per person per day for room and three meals. Group rates are available.

Write or telephone: The Guest Master.

Directions: The friary is near the intersection of Routes 25A, 347, and 83, just about in the middle of Long Island. The friars will provide more detailed directions if needed.

If using public transportation, take the Long Island Railroad from Manhattan (Penn Station). From New England, take the ferry (Bridgeport and Port Jefferson Steamboat Company) from Bridgeport, Connecticut, to Port Jefferson. Arrange in advance for pickup on arrival.

History: This community of Episcopal Franciscan brothers was founded in Wisconsin in 1919 by the Reverend Joseph Crookston. St. Francis and his brethren had a chapel at Portiuncula, and in 1928 an American "Little Portion" was established on Long Island.

Description: The buildings at Little Portion reflect the simple lifestyle of the brothers. The friary is on more than sixty acres, abutting Mt. Sinai Harbor and its wildlife sanctuary.

Points of Interest: Little Portion is in an area that has been designated a historic district.

Mount Saviour Monastery

231 Monastery Road
Pine City, New York 14871-9787

Telephone: (607) 734-1688.

Facsimile: (607) 734-1689.

Order: Benedictine monks (Roman Catholic).

Accommodations: Fifteen men in single rooms (all with shared baths) in St. Joseph's. In addition, there are accommodations for seven women in two twin-bedded and three single rooms in St. Gertrude's. Couples may also stay in St. Gertrude's or in more private facilities at St. Peter's farmhouse, West Casa, or East Casa. Please contact the Guest Brother for more detailed information.

Meals: Three meals daily. Men take meals with the monks in the monastery; women in St. Gertrude's. Private kitchens are available to those staying at St. Peter's farmhouse, East Casa, and West Casa.

Charges: Suggested offering of $40 per night per person. "We are grateful to those who can give more and welcome those whose means allow for less. The generosity of our guests permits us to run the guest houses and we are grateful for their support."

Write, telephone, or fax: The Guest Brother.

Directions: For those driving, Route 17 is the main highway from both east and west. From the east, take the second Elmira exit, marked "Church Street Route 352." Follow Church Street through the city to Route 225. Turn left and continue four miles to Monastery Road on the right. From points west, driving on 17 east, take Exit 45/Route 352 through Corning. Cross the whole town. At the last traffic light, turn right on Route 225. (Be prepared to bear left just after you enter onto this road.) There are two turns, but they are well marked. Continue on 225 until you come to Monastery Road on the left.

Coming from points north or south, Route 14 crosses Church Street (Route 352) in Elmira. Church Street is one-way. Continue on Church Street to Route 225, turn left, and continue to Monastery Road on the right.

For those using public transportation, there is air service to the Elmira/Corning Airport (about ten miles away). There is shuttle service to the monastery for $15. (It is best to call in advance: Southern Tier Express at 607-739-5499.) For those traveling by bus, the same bus terminal in Elmira serves inter-city and local buses. A local bus marked "Golden Glow" stops at Hendy Creek Market on Route 225 four miles from the monastery. If you are arriving before 5:00 P.M., you may make arrangements with the Guest Brother to be met at the Market. If you arrive after 5:00 P.M., please take a cab to the monastery. Although the monastery's mailing address is in Pine City, *do not take the bus marked "Pine City"*. It will not take you to the monastery.

History: Mount Saviour, named in honor of the Saviour's Transfiguration, was established in 1951 by Father Damasus Winzen and three companions.

Description: Atop Mount Saviour are the monastery's octagonal chapel and towering spire. A fourteenth-century statue of the Virgin stands in the center of the chapel's crypt. Beyond the cluster of the chapel and monastery are more than two hundred acres of woodlands and fields.

Points of Interest: The monastery is in the beautiful Finger Lakes region of New York State. Cornell University, the Corning Glass Museum, and Mark Twain's house are nearby.

Special Note: Mount Saviour does not accommodate overnight-only guests; the minimum stay is two days, with most guests staying two to seven days. Group retreats may be given on special request. A brochure and further information may be obtained from the Guest Brother.

Neale House

50 Fulton Street
New York, New York 10038-1800

Telephone: (212) 619-2672. (Best times to call: 9:00 A.M. to 12:00 noon and evenings after 6:00 P.M.)

Order: Society of St. Margaret (Episcopal).

Accommodations: Two guests in the convent in single rooms with shared bath.

Meals: Breakfast only.

Charges: $35 per person for bed and breakfast.

Write or telephone: Sr. Mary Michael, Sister-in-Charge.

Directions: For those driving, Fulton Street is located near Manhattan's southern tip just south of City Hall and east of Broadway.

For those using public transportation, the Fulton Street Subway stop is near Neale House. Several subway routes stop at Fulton Street, including Green 4 and 5, Brown J and Z, Red 2 and 3, and Blue A and C. If you are traveling by city bus from mid-town, buses numbers 1 and 6 will leave you at the corner of Broadway and Fulton Street. As in any major city, if you are uncertain about directions at night or during off-peak hours, it is best to use a taxi or, more specifically in New York, a Yellow Cab.

History: Founded in England in 1854, the Society of St. Margaret arrived in the United States in 1873. The sisters at Neale House are engaged in pastoral work at Trinity Church, Wall Street. Often referred to as the "Mother of Churches," Trinity was the first Anglican parish in New York City, having been granted a charter by King William III in 1697. The present church, considered to be one of Richard Upjohn's finest works, was completed in 1846. It is hard to imagine that Trinity's spire was the tallest structure in Manhattan for fifty years. An adjunct of Trinity, and another ministry of the sisters, is St. Paul's Chapel at Broadway and Fulton Street. Inspired by the design for London's St. Martin-in-the-Fields and built in the 1760s, it is the oldest church standing on Manhattan Island.

Points of Interest: Neale House is close to City Hall (1803), the entrance to the Brooklyn Bridge with pedestrian walk, and Chinatown. Farther south are the South Street Seaport Museum, Wall Street with the stock exchanges, Federal Hall National Memorial, the Smithsonian's National Museum of the American Indian, and Battery Park, where one may embark on a ferry ride to the Statue of Liberty and Ellis Island.

St. Cuthbert's House and St. Aidan's House

Melrose
R.D. 13
Federal Hill Road
Brewster, New York 10509

Telephone: (914) 278-2610 or (914) 278-4854.

Order: Community of the Holy Spirit (Episcopal).

Accommodations: Eighteen guests in two guest houses in single and twin rooms, two of which have private baths.

Meals: Three meals daily.

Charges: $55 per person per night for room and three meals or $40 per person per night for bed and breakfast only.

Write or telephone: The Sister-in-Charge.

Directions: If driving from New York City, take the Saw Mill River Parkway or I-87 or I-684 at White Plains. From points west or north, take I-84 or Route 6 (both will bypass Brewster proper to Route 22). Bypassing Brewster, I-684 becomes Route 22. Proceed as to Pawling. Pass Heidi's Motel on the right and continue about a half mile to a large "New Fairfield" sign on the right, up a small incline. Get into the far right lane. At the traffic light, take Mill Town Road; after about .8 mile, you pass an old cemetery on the left, go down a slight decline, and cross a low bridge. At once the road divides. Do not take the left fork (New Fairfield Road). Take the right fork, Federal Hill Road, one-fifth of a mile up the hill to Melrose.

From New England and points east, take Route 7 (Connecticut) or I-84 to Danbury. Bypass Danbury, continuing west on I-84 to Exit 2. Leave I-84 and turn right onto Old #6 (Mill-Plain Road). Continue east one-quarter mile to a large, new office building on the right (and pizza/deli on the left). Turn left onto Aunt Hack's Road, but do not take this road as it goes sharply uphill, and do not take the Mill-Plain Road that goes sharply to the left. Instead, take Joe's Hill Road (between these two roads). There is a Melrose School sign posted on a tree at this junction. Follow this road two miles to the Connecticut border (and a small pond) at the top of the hill. Continue on this road for .6 mile to Melrose on the left. The entrance to the retreat house is around the back.

If using public transportation from Manhattan, take the Metro North train to Brewster, New York, or bus service to Danbury, Connecticut. From local airports there is limousine service to Danbury, Connecticut.

History: St. Cuthbert's House was founded in 1972.

Description: St. Cuthbert's is a white clapboard house dating back to 1743, later topped with a mansard roof. The house includes a dining room and a living room area with a fireplace, and an adjacent small chapel. Both houses include areas for small group meetings. St. Cuthbert's, St. Aidan's, and the convent are surrounded by woodlands and hills.

Special Note: A full schedule of group retreats is offered at Melrose. A calendar and further information are available from the Sister-in-Charge.

St. Hilda's House

621 West 113th Street
New York, New York 10025-7916

Telephone: (212) 932-8098.

Order: Community of the Holy Spirit (Episcopal).

Accommodations: Twenty guests in the convent in fourteen single rooms (with shared baths), two double-bedded rooms (with private baths), and one twin-bedded room (with shared bath). No accommodations for guests on Mondays.

Meals: Daily with the sisters, with prior arrangement.

Charges: $50 per person per night for room. No additional charges for meals.

Write or telephone: The Assistant Hospitality Coordinator.

Directions: If driving, call the convent for specific directions from your starting point.

For those using public transportation, there is the Public Carey Bus from JFK International Airport to Grand Central Station (in midtown Manhattan). By subway from Grand Central Station, take the number 1 or number 9 train to 110th Street. Then walk north to 113th Street and west (left) to the convent. Alternately, from midtown Manhattan, take the M4 bus or the M104 bus up Broadway to 112th Street. Walk one block north to 113th Street, then west (left) to the convent. From LaGuardia Airport, take bus M60 to Broadway and 116th Street. Then walk south to 113th Street and right to the convent.

History: The foundress of the Community of the Holy Spirit was the Reverend Mother Ruth. The child of an interracial marriage, Ruth Elaine Younger joined an Anglican Canadian sisterhood in the 1920s. In 1949, Sr. Ruth returned to her native New York City. Uncompromising and dynamic, she founded a school and, in 1952, the Community of the Holy Spirit.

The community has enlarged its ministries to include a full program of guest hospitality, conducted retreats, art exhibits, poetry/fiction readings, concerts, chaplaincy work in hospitals and nursing homes, and special programs in parishes. Some of the sisters are experienced in crafts, needlework, and icon painting. Their work is available in the gift shop or by special order.

Points of Interest: "Located in Manhattan's Upper West Side, the many sights and experiences of New York City are readily available. Many guests and visitors have expressed appreciation for the ability to experience the rich heritage of the city and the peace and stillness of the convent—a 'haven in the city.'"

Special Note: Please contact the convent for a copy of *Outpourings*, its schedule of retreats, workshops, and cultural events.

St. Margaret's House

Jordan Road
New Hartford, New York 13413

Telephone: (315) 724-2324.

Order: Society of St. Margaret (Episcopal).

Accommodations: Sixteen guests (twelve women and four men) in single rooms in the retreat house, all with shared bath.

Meals: Three meals daily.

Charges: $35 per person per day for room and meals.

Write or telephone: The Guest Sister.

Directions: If driving on the New York State Thruway (I-87), take the New Hartford exit south to Route 8, then right on Route 5 (Genesee Street) and left on Jordan Road.

For those using public transportation, there are plane, train, and bus services to Utica.

History: John Mason Neale, a priest of the Church of England, author, and hymn writer, founded the Society of St. Margaret in 1854. In 1873 three sisters were sent to America to work at the Children's Hospital in Boston. The American branch of the society numbers about fifty members today, who live and work at the motherhouse in Massachusetts and at four Mission Houses. The sisters in New Hartford are involved in urban and retreat ministries.

Description: St. Margaret's House is set on ten acres of land just south of the city of Utica. The convent and chapel are surrounded by lawns, trees, and gardens.

Special Note: In addition to opportunities for individuals to have private retreats, group retreats are also offered here. Information may be obtained from the Guest Sister.

St. Mary's Convent

John Street
Peekskill, New York 10566

Telephone: (914) 737-0113.

Facsimile: (914) 737-4019.

Order: Community of St. Mary (Episcopal).

Accommodations: Up to twenty guests in St. Benedict's Retreat House and in St. Gabriel's Retreat House. Most rooms are single, a few twin and (with sofa bed) triple.

Meals: Meals are taken in silence and are provided for guests staying in St. Benedict's.

Charges: Suggested contribution of $35 per person per day for room and meals; $25 per day for longer visits.

Write, telephone, or fax: The Guest Mistress.

Directions: For those driving, directions and a map are available from the convent on request.

If using public transportation from Manhattan (Grand Central Station), take the train to Peekskill. This will be about an hour's journey. Then take a taxi to the convent, "but depending on time and available cars, sometimes we can meet trains."

History: The first religious community in the Episcopal Church, the convent was founded by Harriet Starr Canon and four companions in 1865 in New York City. In 1873 it was moved to Peekskill. From the beginning, the community has been involved in a number of works at schools, hospitals, missions and retreat houses. The making of altar breads is included among the community's works.

Description: The convent, built in 1902 of granite quarried on the property, sits within a lovely landscaped setting on the banks of the Hudson River.

Special Note: Contact the Guest Mistress for a brochure and a schedule of group retreats. Group bookings are limited to twenty guests.

The Leo House

332 West 23rd Street
New York, New York 10011-2289

Telephone: (800) 732-2438 (800-621-4667 from Canada) or (212) 929-1010. (Best time to call: 8:00 A.M. to 11:00 P.M.)

Facsimile: (212) 366-6801.

Order: Sisters of St. Agnes (Roman Catholic).

Accommodations: Up to one hundred guests in sixty rooms. Rooms are single, twin-bedded, double-bedded, or family (i.e., one queen-sized bed, two twin beds, and, on request, two cots, for a total occupancy of six). Some rooms have full bath; others have a sink and toilet with shared showers.

Meals: Buffet breakfast Monday through Saturday; continental breakfast on Sundays.

Charges: Room rates range from $59 for a single room with shared shower to $140 for six in the family room with private bath.

Write, telephone, or fax: The Reservation Desk.

Directions: If driving, keep in mind that 23rd Street is a two-way street running east and west across midtown Manhattan. The Leo House is located on 23rd Street between Eighth and Ninth Avenues.

For those using public transportation, the Grey Line Air Shuttle Bus will transport travelers from area airports to the door of the Leo House for a fee of about $18. An alternative from the airports is the Carey Bus to Grand Central Station, and then a taxi (be advised to hire only a Yellow Cab). If arriving by train at Grand Central Station or Penn Station, or by bus at the Port Authority Bus Terminal, it is a short Yellow Cab ride to the Leo House. If using the city bus, take the Seventh Avenue bus (#10) southbound to 23rd Street. If traveling by subway, take the Eighth Avenue line (Red number 1, 2, 3, or 9) to the 23rd Street Station. It is a half-block walk from the subway exit/entrance to the Leo House.

History: The Leo House, opened in 1889, is named in honor of Pope Leo XIII. A Catholic nonprofit organization, the house was begun by the St. Raphael Society, and later staffed by the Sisters of St. Agnes, to help newly-arrived German immigrants. Leo-Haus, as it was originally known, moved from the Battery Park neighborhood at the southern tip of Manhattan to its present home in the 1920s. Though the wave of German immigrants has subsided, the hospitality offered here has not. To this day the Leo House offers temporary accommodation to "priests, religious, relatives of hospitalized persons, [and] international and domestic travelers. Its safe, simple, and clean accommodations are suited to guests on a modest budget…. People of all faiths are welcome."

Description: Built in 1926, the Leo House is an eight-story building complete with a comfortably and tastefully furnished lobby, a chapel, a cafeteria, and meeting rooms. "Within the noise and rush of the city, Leo House is a haven for those… seeking rest and reflection in their travels."

Points of Interest: Centrally located, the Leo House has as its neighbors midtown to the north, and to the south, Greenwich Village, Little Italy, Chinatown, Tribeca, the Lower East Side, and the Financial District.

Transfiguration Monastery

R.D. #2, Box 2612
Windsor, New York 13865

Telephone: (607) 655-2366.

Order: Camaldolese/Benedictine nuns (Roman Catholic).

Accommodations: Eight guests in the guest house. There are four single rooms, one twin, and one sitting/bedroom, all with shared bath.

Meals: Three meals daily.

Charges: $30 to $35 per person per day.

Write or telephone: Sr. Jeanne Marie Pearse, Guest Sister.

Directions: If driving, take Route 17 to Exit 79 (Windsor), then south three-and-one-half miles on Route 79. The monastery will be on the right, just before the golf course.

For those using public transportation, there is bus service to Binghamton, New York.

History: Two Benedictine nuns (Sr. Mary Placid Deliard and Sr. Jeanne Marie Pearse) were accepted into the Roman Catholic Diocese of Syracuse in 1975 to establish a Benedictine monastery. They were later joined by Sr. Donald Corcoran, and the three nuns acquired a suitable property in New York's Southern Tier, where they have built their simple and attractive monastery. In 1988 the community affiliated with the Camaldolese—a congregation of the Benedictine order. Begun by St. Romuald in eleventh-century Italy, Camaldolese monasteries provide for the monastic life-style lived both in community and in hermitages.

Description: Transfiguration Monastery is set on one hundred acres of woodland and arable river plain nestled at the foot of Horeb Mountain (the "Mountain of God"). Reflecting the nuns' simplicity of spirit and concern for ecology, the monastery is built with natural materials such as wood and stone. Passive solar energy and woodburning stoves are used.

Kanuga

Postal Drawer 250
Hendersonville, North Carolina 28793

Telephone: (704) 692-9136. (Best time to call: Monday through Friday 9:00 A.M. to 5:00 P.M.)

Facsimile: (704) 696-3589.

Order: Affiliated with the Episcopal Church.

Accommodations: Up to 440 guests in the inn, cottages, and guest houses in single and twin-bedded rooms, some of which have private baths.

Meals: Three meals daily.

Charges: $80.50 per person per day for room and three meals, single occupancy, and $65.50 per person per day for room and three meals, double occupancy.

Write, telephone, or fax: Ray F. West, Jr., Vice President for Administration.

Directions: If driving from US Interstate 26, take Exit 18-B on US 64 West into Hendersonville. Turn left on US 25 south (Church Street) and drive nine blocks. Turn right on Kanuga Street, go four miles to the Kanuga triangular sign. Turn right, drive one-and-one-half miles to Kanuga Entrance Park. Then turn right and drive a half mile.

For those using public transportation, there is air service (U.S. Airways and Delta) to Asheville Regional Airport, and then ground transportation (rental car or limousine) to Kanuga. There is also Greyhound bus service to Hendersonville.

History: The Kanuga Lake Club Resort opened its doors in 1909. This was originally a private resort where visitors lodged in traditional cottages overlooking the thirty-acre Lake Kanuga. In 1928, sponsored by three Episcopal dioceses in the Carolinas, Kanuga became a summer camp and, later, a conference center. The pine frame Chapel of the Transfiguration was begun in 1938 and dedicated in 1942. Kanuga Lake Inn was built in 1968 to accommodate year-round visitors, and more recently (1979–1984) six guest houses were added that blend into the mountain setting. Today Kanuga attracts over twenty-five thousand visitors annually.

Description: The chapel is the "Heart of Kanuga," constructed of pine trees that fell during a 1936 storm. Its architect was S. Grant Alexander, O.B.E., a Scotsman who made North Carolina his home. A place of rustic beauty and inspiration, the Chapel of the Transfiguration is as well known in the worldwide Anglican Communion as its greatest cathedrals and shrines. Among others, Anglican leaders have spoken and worshiped here.

The original thirty-nine cottages are attractively rustic, roomy, and well furnished. Kanuga Lake Inn is a more modern lodge built of mountain fieldstone. Porches and patios (both private and public) overlook the lake, and there are a lounge with a fireplace, a library, dining rooms, and St. John's Chapel. Kanuga's newest additions—six guest cottages—also have porches, and living rooms with fireplaces. Recreational facilities include tennis courts, a croquet lawn, a gymnasium, and a lakefront pavilion. All of this is set on fourteen hundred acres in the breathtakingly beautiful mountains of western North Carolina. Guests are free to explore the woodlands, ridges, valleys, and streams.

Points of Interest: Kanuga is close to Asheville, where one may visit the magnificent Biltmore Estate and the Thomas Wolfe Homestead. Not far away are the Carl Sandburg National Historic Site, the Blue Ridge Parkway, Great Smoky Mountains National Park, and views from the summit of Mt. Mitchell, the highest elevation east of the Rockies.

Special Note: Kanuga offers many programs every year, including conferences and meetings, summer camps, guest periods/vacation times, parish family weekends, a mountain-trail outdoor school, retreats, leadership training and educational programs, and personal interest and hobby groups. Kanuga publishes an annual program catalog, which is available on request.

Assumption Abbey

Post Office Box A
Richardton, North Dakota 58652

Telephone: (701) 974-3315. (Best times to call: 8:00 A.M. to
11:30 A.M. and 12:30 P.M. to 4:30 P.M.)

Facsimile: (701) 974-3317.

Order: Benedictine monks (Roman Catholic).

Accommodations: One hundred guests in single rooms, seven of
which have private baths.

Meals: Three meals daily.

Charges: $10 for room and $15 for meals per person per day.

Write, telephone, or fax: The Guest Master.

Directions: If driving from Bismark, take Interstate Highway 94 seventy-five miles west to Richardton.

For those using public transportation, there is Greyhound bus service to Richardton. Please contact the Guest Master for further directions.

History: Assumption Abbey has its roots in Switzerland. In 1888 monks from Einsiedeln Abbey came to the Dakota Territory and at first settled in Devil's Lake. In 1899 they arrived in Richardton to minister to the German immigrants who had settled in southwestern North Dakota. By 1911 the abbey church, the monastic quadrangle, and other buildings serving the community were completed. Today Assumption Abbey is home base to sixty-five monks, of whom thirty are on mission to Indians and others in North Dakota, in several other states, and in South America.

Description: The massive abbey church was designed in the Bavarian Romanesque style, its interior delineated by lofty arches. Fifty-two stained-glass windows light the interior, its nave guarded by twenty-four saints depicted on canvas. Beyond the church are a pottery, a printshop and book bindery, a communications center, a woodcraft shop, an apiary, and a two thousand-acre ranch with three hundred head of cattle. Guests may wish to walk to the surrounding open fields, woods, and the serene Abbey Lake.

St. Andrew Svorad Abbey

10510 Buckeye Road
Cleveland, Ohio 44104-3725

Telephone: (216) 721-5300. (Best times to call: Monday through Friday 8:30 A.M. to 7:30 P.M., and Saturdays and Sundays 9:00 A.M. to 7:00 P.M.)

Facsimile: (216) 791-8268.

Order: Benedictine monks (Roman Catholic).

Accommodations: Up to ten guests in the guest quarters wing of the monastery in single and twin-bedded rooms, all with private baths.

Meals: Three meals daily.

Charges: Freewill offering.

Write, telephone, or fax: Brother Ignatius Issac, O.S.B., the Guest Master.

Directions: If driving from points east on Interstate 80 (Ohio Turnpike), take the interchange to Interstate 480 northbound. This will merge with Interstate 271. Continue on Interstate 271 and exit at Chagrin Boulevard. Go left off the ramp to Richmond Road and turn right onto Richmond Road to Shaker Boulevard, turning left (Shaker Boulevard has a wide median dividing east- and westbound traffic. Cross eastbound Shaker Boulevard in order to turn left onto Shaker Boulevard westbound). Continue west-bound on Shaker Boulevard for approximately five-and-one-half to six miles to Martin Luther King Drive. Turn left onto the drive (moving to the right lane). Just beyond the second traffic light, on the right, there is a church on the corner, followed by the Benedictine High School. Between these two buildings is the abbey driveway. Turn right onto the property. There is parking in front of the abbey church.

If traveling east on Interstate 90 toward downtown Cleveland, you will cross Interstate 71. Continue east on I-90, it will become I-490, ending at East 55th Street. If traveling north on Interstate 71 or Interstate 77 toward downtown Cleveland, take I-490 eastbound until it ends at East 55th Street. Turn left onto East 55th Street (northbound) for a half mile. Turn right onto Woodland Avenue (eastbound) for one mile. Turn right onto Buckeye Road (eastbound). Stay on Buckeye Road one mile. Turn right onto Martin Luther King Jr. Drive and follow the directions given above.

If using public transportation, take rapid transit lines 67X (Van Aken-Blue Line) or 67AX (Shaker-Green Line). Alternately, take bus Routes 10, 11, or 13 (Woodhill Road) or Route 50 (East 116th Street).

History: St. Andrew's Abbey was founded by members of the Roman Catholic Slovak-American community. In 1922 Slovak monks from the predominately Czech St. Procopius Abbey (Illinois) assumed leadership at St. Andrew's Parish in Cleveland. By 1929 the Cleveland priory was independent and was then raised to the status of an abbey in 1934. As the community and its works grew, so did its physical plant. Today St. Andrew's Abbey, an enduring and inspiring presence in urban Cleveland, is home to approximately fifty monks who live the Benedictine ideal of "work and prayer" at the abbey, at the Benedictine High School, in parishes, and in various chaplaincies.

Description: The abbey is located in the Buckeye-Woodland neighborhood of southeast Cleveland on sixteen wooded acres at a high point overlooking the city.

Points of Interest: The neighborhood surrounding the abbey has a large Hungarian population. Of particular note is St. Elizabeth's Church, the oldest Hungarian Catholic Church in America. About one mile north of St. Andrew's is the largest cluster of cultural institutions in the country, including Cleveland's Institute of Art, Institute of Music, Museum of Art, Clinic, and Orchestra (at Severance Hall), Case Western Reserve University, the Western Reserve Historical Society, and other museums, hospitals, and notable churches of many denominations.

Osage Monastery

Forest of Peace
18701 West Monastery Road
Sand Springs, Oklahoma 74063-5300

Telephone: (918) 245-2734. (Best time to call: 9:00 A.M. to 12:00 noon.)

Facsimile: (918) 245-9360.

Order: Benedictine Sisters of Perpetual Adoration (Roman Catholic).

Accommodations: Six guests in one-room cabins, each with private shower.

Meals: Three meals daily (vegetarian).

Charges: There is no set fee.

Write, telephone, or fax: Sister Helen.

Directions: If driving from Tulsa, take Highway 64 west toward Sand Springs. Four miles past Sand Springs, exit at 177 West Avenue. Turn right (north). Go one mile to Anderson Road and turn left (west). Then go one mile to Shell Creek West subdivision and turn right on Ridge Avenue. Go one block to Lakeview Drive (a white gravel road between two houses). Turn right (north) and follow the road to a sign reading "Monastery Road." Turn right (east) and enter the monastery parking lot under the trees.

If driving from Oklahoma City, take I-44 east toward Tulsa. At Sapulpa, take Highway 97 north to Sand Springs. Take Highway 64 west to 177 West Avenue. Then continue as above.

There is no public transportation available.

History: For more than 120 years the Benedictine Sisters of Perpetual Adoration have been dedicated to the monastic tradition of prayer and work. In 1980, the sesquimillennium year of St. Benedict's birth, Osage Monastery was dedicated. Often called "O+M", the monastery is located in Osage County, home of the Osage Indians—hence its name: Osage+Monastery. O+M, taken from the monastery's two initials flanking Christ's cross, form the sacred word for God in the Far East: OM.

Description: (As described by one of the sisters): "Fourteen one-room cabins for community and ashramites surround the chapel, the heart of the monastery. Two of the chapel walls are glass, through which one can see the gentle oak trees gathered, standing through the seasons in their own silent vigil. The floor is hardwood with a circular sunken center, linking prayers there to kivas and medicine wheels and mandalas throughout space and time. A transparent tabernacle hangs on one side of the sanctuary, bringing Christ's presence into awareness, while symbols of Native American, Hindu, Jewish and Buddhist traditions hang on the walls, reminding all of the many faces and epiphanies of the Divine."

Special Note: The sisters produce and sell pottery and liturgical stoles and publish an intermonastic East-West bulletin three times annually, which is "sent to the four corners of the world."

Trappist Abbey of Our Lady of Guadalupe

Post Office Box 97
Lafayette, Oregon 97127

Telephone: (503) 852-0107. (Best times to call: 8:00 A.M. to 7:00 P.M.)

Facsimile: (503) 852-7748.

Order: Cistercian (Trappist) monks (Roman Catholic).

Accommodations: Four men and four women in single rooms in the guest house, with two rooms per bath.

Meals: Three meals daily.

Charges: $20 per person per day.

Write, telephone, or fax: The Guest Master.

Directions: If driving from Portland, drive south on Interstate 5 to the Tigard/Highway 99W exit. Turn right and stay on Highway 99W for twenty-six miles to Lafayette. In Lafayette, drive to the west end. Turn off 99W onto Bridge Street (sign also says "Trappist Abbey") and go north three miles, staying on the surface road. The abbey is on the right.

If using public transportation, contact the Guest Master for directions.

History: The Cistercian Order dates back to the Abbey of Citeaux (near Dijon, France), which was founded in 1098 by monks who wished to live the Rule of St. Benedict in greater poverty, seclusion, and strictness than were customary at that time. The work of St. Bernard of Clairvaux in 1115 started an enormous expansion of the Cistercian Order throughout Europe. The name "Trappist" is derived from the Cistercian Abbey of La Trappe in Normandy, France. La Trappe was reformed in the late seventeenth century. In 1790, when all French religious houses were suppressed because of the French Revolution, the community of La Trappe took refuge in Switzerland, returning to its monastery in 1815. Subsequently, the congregation flourished. Today there are about one hundred Trappist monasteries of men and sixty of women throughout the world.

Our Lady of Guadalupe Abbey began in 1948 at Pecos, New Mexico. As this was not an ideal location for the farming they wished to pursue, the monks relocated to Oregon in 1955.

The abbey's patron, Our Lady of Guadalupe, "was chosen because of the Mexican influence in the Southwest, but was gladly brought along to the Northwest." Today the abbey numbers nearly fifty monks, ranging in age from the twenties to the nineties.

Description: The abbey is set amid ponds, farm fields, tall pines, and other trees. Bethany House, the new guest house, has a contemporary design. Constructed of wood, it has warm interiors with wide windows looking out onto the surrounding woodlands.

Community of Celebration

809 Franklin Avenue
Post Office Box 309
Aliquippa, Pennsylvania 15001

Telephone: (412) 375-1510. (Best time to call: Monday through Friday 9:00 A.M. to 5:00 P.M.)

Facsimile: (412) 375-1138.

Order: Community of Celebration (Episcopal).

Accommodations: Four guests in two twin-bedded rooms, all sharing a single full bath, living room, and large kitchen.

Meals: Breakfast is provided, and self-prepared, in the guest house kitchen. Depending on prior arrangements, lunch may be self-prepared or eaten with one of the community's households. Most evening meals are shared with community households, unless otherwise arranged.

Charges: $25 per person per day for room and board.

Write, telephone, or fax: The Guest Mistress, Rose Krupansky.

Directions: If driving from points east, take Interstate 80 and exit onto Interstate 79, southbound. Follow 79 to the Sewickley exit. Exit to the right. At the bottom of the ramp, turn left at the stop sign; this road will cross back under 79. At the next stop sign turn right; ramp takes you onto Route 65. Follow 65 to Ambridge. You will pass through business sections of Sewickley and Leetsdale and then come to Ambridge. Soon you will be able to see a bridge to the left (Ambridge Bridge); when you get to the traffic light before the bridge, turn right. Go about two blocks and turn left at the next light. This is Maplewood Avenue in Ambridge. Follow road to the next traffic light and turn left. The Ambridge Bridge will be in front of you. Cross the bridge and turn right to get onto Route 51. Follow 51 and get off at the first exit to the right, Aliquippa. The ramp will come to a T. Turn left. Go through two traffic lights. Just beyond the third traffic light and on the left side are the community's office and row houses.

If driving from points west, take Interstate 80 to Route 60, south- or eastbound. Follow signs that indicate Pittsburgh International Airport, even though you will exit before the airport. (There are several toll booths near the beginning of 60.) Stay on 60 to the Aliquippa exit (which comes after the exit for "Center"). Exit to the right. The ramp continues to the right onto a four-lane road. Stay on this road through three traffic lights. (These lights are not close together.) The road will curve, go through a business section, and pass an elementary school on the right before the third light. About a half mile after the third light, look for the road to split—one lane will go straight and the other lane will curve to the right; this is Franklin Avenue. Follow the lane to the right. Continue on this road past several blocks of houses on the left and a large church, also on the left. The community's row houses are ahead on the right side; they have barn red top-floor dormers.

For those using public transportation, Pittsburgh International Airport is a fifteen-minute drive from Aliquippa. Guests can often be met on arrival with prior arrangement. From the city of Pittsburgh (twenty miles away) there is bus service. Contact the Guest Mistress for more detailed directions.

History: The Society of the Community of Celebration, first established in England and Scotland, has its American roots in Houston, Texas. There an "extended family" Christian life-style was adopted by many as early as 1965. Formally established in 1972, the community resettled in Aliquippa in 1985—a once thriving steel town—to work and pray for the regeneration of the town's economy, environment, and social and spiritual health. Differing from traditional monastic orders, the community's membership includes men and women, married and single, adults and children, clergy and laity. They do, however, take traditional Benedictine vows, and live simply on subsistence salaries and under the authority of the community's chapter.

Description: The community owns a series of three-story brick row houses and a separate house with a chapel, meeting room, and office space. The row house properties have been developed to maximize green space; the backyards of twelve houses are combined into an expansive lawn—an open, green refuge in an otherwise decaying urban environment.

Points of Interest: Just across the river from Aliquippa is Ambridge, the site of Old Economy Village. The village was the home of the Harmonists, a nineteenth-century Christian communal society best known for its piety and industrial prosperity. Trinity Episcopal School for Ministry is also located in Ambridge. Farther afield, just forty minutes southeast, is Pittsburgh with its numerous cultural amenities, museums, planetariums, IMAX theater, riverboat cruises, and professional and collegiate sporting events year-round.

Special Note: The community sells worship resources (books, sheet music, recordings, videos, cards, and more) through its mail-order catalog.

St. Anna's Convent

2016 Race Street
Philadelphia, Pennsylvania 19103

Telephone: (215) 567-2943. (Best time to call: 10:00 A.M. to 7:00 P.M.)

Order: All Saints Sisters of the Poor (Episcopal).

Accommodations: Eighteen guests in the convent in fourteen single and two double rooms, all with shared baths.

Meals: Light breakfast only.

Charges: Donations.

Write or telephone: The Sister-in-Charge.

Directions: For those driving, St. Anna's is located in center city near Logan Circle on Race Street (one-way eastbound) between 20th Street (northbound) and 21st Street (southbound). The Franklin Institute, across the street from St. Anna's, permits nightly parking at a reduced rate.

If using public transportation and traveling on Amtrak, be sure to get off at the 30th Street Station. Then take a cab the short distance to the convent. For those arriving by bus, the short cab ride is suggested.

History: Begun in England in 1856, the All Saints Sisters of the Poor came to the United States in 1872. Their American motherhouse is in Catonsville, Maryland, just outside of Baltimore.

Description: St. Anna's is a handsome red brick house, typical of those built in Philadelphia. There are a chapel and a sitting room for the use of guests. The All Saints Sisters are a very traditional order. This is reflected in their convent life and, more visibly, in their traditional full religious habit, complete with starched white wimple and black veil, which they continue to wear to this day.

Points of Interest: St. Anna's is virtually on the doorsteps of St. Clement's Episcopal Church, a bastion of traditional Anglo-Catholic worship; the Roman Catholic Cathedral of Sts. Peter and Paul (1846), a replica of Rome's St. Peter's Basilica; the Franklin Institute, with its scientific exhibits; and, farther up the Parkway, the Philadelphia Museum of Art. Near Independence Hall (1732) are the Episcopal churches of Gloria Dei/Old Swede's (1700), St. Peter's (1761), and Christ Church (1727). St. Mary's Roman Catholic Church (1763), Old Pine Street Presbyterian Church (1764), and the Friends Meeting House (1804) are also located in the area.

St. Emma Monastery and Retreat House

1001 Harvey Avenue
Greensburg, Pennsylvania 15601-1494

Telephone: (412) 834-3060. (Best times to call: 8:00 A.M. to 11:30 A.M. and 2:00 P.M. to 4:30 P.M.)

Facsimile: (412) 834-5772.

Order: Sisters of St. Benedict (Roman Catholic).

Accommodations: Fifty-four guests in the retreat house, each in a single room with sink, and all with shared baths.

Meals: Three meals daily.

Charges: $40 per person per day for room and meals.

Write, telephone, or fax: Mother Mary Anne, O.S.B., Prioress.

Directions: If driving, take the Pennsylvania Turnpike (I-76) to Exit 6. Pick up US 22 east to PA 819 south. It is a five-mile drive on route PA 819 to the monastery.

For those using public transportation, there are Amtrak and bus (Westmoreland Transit) services to Greensburg. It is then a two-mile taxicab ride to the monastery. For those arriving by air, there is a USAirways commuter plane from Pittsburgh International Airport to Latrobe Airport. Taxis and rental cars are available at the airport.

History: St. Emma's Monastery has its roots in the nine hundred-year-old St. Walburg Abbey, Eichstaett, Bavaria. It was in 1931 that Mother M. Leonarda Fritz, accompanied by nine sisters, arrived in western Pennsylvania. There they worked and cooked at St. Vincent's Archabbey, seminary, college, and prep school in Latrobe. By working in Latrobe the sisters were able to save their earnings and send them "home" to St. Walburg Abbey and to help other budding communities as well. During World War II communications between the States and Germany were impaired, but in 1943, by way of Canada, the sisters received word from Eichstaett to "look out for yourselves." This they interpreted to mean "buy your own property," and that they did in a beautiful country setting.

In the 1950s a chapel was built on the property, followed by the monastery and retreat house (1960) and many thoughtful additions since. It is interesting to note that in the early 1960s, St. Emma's helped pioneer the use of English in the daily office (the second community of Benedictine sisters in the United States to do so), though they still sing the traditional Gregorian chants to this day.

Description: Immediately surrounding the monastery are ten well-manicured acres and an outdoor Stations of the Cross winding through an apple orchard. There is a twelve-foot-high Crucifixion group overlooking the cemetery. Beyond are ninety acres of farm-land and rolling hills. Guests can visit the Fatima, Blessed Sacrament, and Sacred Heart Chapels, where daily services are sung. St. Walburga Shrine at the monastery is an exceptionally beautiful chapel, with a series of ten old stained-glass windows depicting the life of the eighth-century Benedictine nun and missionary to Germany.

Points of Interest: St. Vincent's Archabbey, founded by Bavarian monks in 1846, is just twelve miles from St. Emma's. In 1996, during the abbey's 150th anniversary year, the massive and venerable abbey church was renovated.

St. Margaret's House

5419 Germantown Avenue
Philadelphia, Pennsylvania 19144

Telephone: (215) 844-9410.

Order: Society of St. Margaret (Episcopal).

Accommodations: Up to sixteen guests in the Mission House. Three rooms are twin, the others single, and all have shared bath.

Meals: Three meals daily.

Charges: Suggested donation of $35 per person per night.

Write or telephone: The Guest Sister.

Directions: If driving, take the New Jersey Turnpikee to the Pennsylvania Turnpike. Take Exit 26 (Fort Washington), then Route 309 south to the Mt. Airy exit. Continue straight ahead and then go left onto Germantown Avenue. Continue on Germantown Avenue for about two miles until you get to St. Luke's Church (on your left). Turn into the driveway; St. Margaret's House is the first building on the left.

For those using public transportation, there is Greyhound and Trailways bus services to Philadelphia, as well as Amtrak train service. From downtown Philadelphia at Suburban Station (J. F. Kennedy Boulevard and 16th Street), take the Chestnut Hill West train to Chelten Avenue Station (in Germantown). This will be a seventeen-minute ride. Call St. Margaret's House and someone will drive over to pick you up.

History: The Sisters of St. Margaret have been in the Episcopal Diocese of Pennsylvania for more than a century. St. Margaret's House has served the diocese as a retreat and conference center since 1939.

Description: This beautiful stone house was built in 1894. It is on the grounds of the historic St. Luke's Episcopal Church, Germantown.

Points of Interest: Germantown is a part of historic Philadelphia. Independence Hall and other downtown sights are easily accessible by local commuter rail.

Special Note: Individuals and group retreats are welcomed each year from after Labor Day until May (usually not from June through August). Further information and a schedule of retreats and quiet days may be obtained from the Guest Sister.

Portsmouth Abbey

Cory's Lane
Portsmouth, Rhode Island 02871

Telephone: (401) 683-2000.

Order: Benedictine monks (Roman Catholic).

Accommodations: Seven men in the monastery in single rooms, one with private bath.

Meals: Three meals daily.

Charges: "Guests who can are asked to make an offering—$20 to $25 a day is suggested."

Write or telephone: The Guest Master.

Directions: If driving from the greater Boston area, take Route 128 south to Route 24 south. Continue on Route 24 until it merges with and becomes Route 114. Continue south for a short distance; Cory's Lane will be on your right.

From Providence take 195 east to Fall River, then take Route 24 south. Continue as with directions from Boston.

From the New York City and southern Connecticut area, take I-95 through Connecticut and pick up Route 138 east in Hope Valley, Rhode Island. Continue east over the Jamestown Bridge to Newport, then take Route 114 north to Portsmouth. As you approach the abbey, there will be a large green sign on the right for "Portsmouth Abbey and School." Cory's Lane is just ahead on the left.

If using public transportation from Boston, take a Bonanza bus to the Town Hall, Portsmouth. If traveling from Providence, take a Rhode Island Public Transit bus to Cory's Lane.

History: Leonard Sargent, monk of Downside Abbey and former member of the Episcopal Order of the Holy Cross, founded this monastery of the English Benedictine Congregation in 1918. He was joined by other monks, Dom Hugh Diman among them. Dom Hugh had been an Episcopal deacon and the founder of St. George's School, Middletown, Rhode Island. In 1926 he opened a second prep school at Portsmouth Priory. The priory became an abbey in 1969.

Description: The abbey property, protected by a cross-topped hill on one side and placid Narragansett Bay on the other, includes five hundred acres of woods, farmland, fields, and landscaped campus. Nestled by the bay is the manor house. This summer cottage, an 1860s Upjohn design, housed the original priory. The new monastery and church were completed in 1960.

Points of Interest: The Green Animals, the best topiary garden in America, is right across the lane from the abbey, and Newport's sights (historic churches, mansions, and Ocean Drive) are just seven miles down the road.

St. Paul's Priory
61 Narragansett Avenue
Newport, Rhode Island 02840

Telephone: (401) 847-2423.

Facsimile: (401) 847-3897.

Order: Benedictines of Jesus Crucified (Roman Catholic).

Accommodations: Nine guests in three twin rooms and three single rooms. Two of the single rooms have private baths.

Meals: The refrigerator is stocked; guests prepare their own meals.

Charges: Please contact the Guest Mistress regarding the suggested donation.

Write, telephone, or fax: The Guest Mistress.

Directions: If driving from Connecticut, New York, or points west take Route 95 through New London into Rhode Island. Take Exit 13 east, then Route 138 east. Follow the signs to the Jamestown and Newport Bridges, taking Route 1 north. Take the first exit to Newport after the Newport Bridge (toll), then make a right onto Farewell Street. At the second stoplight, make a right onto America's Cup Avenue. Continue *straight* onto Thames Street and then left onto Narragansett Avenue.

From Boston and points north, take Route 3 (Southeast Expressway) to Route 128 south (road heads west) to Route 24 south to Newport. Route 24 will merge with Route 114. This becomes Broadway in Newport. Make a left onto America's Cup Avenue, continue *straight* into Thames Street, and make a left onto Narragansett Avenue. The priory will provide a map on request.

For those using public transportation, there are shuttle services from the Boston and Providence airports to the bus station on America's Cup Avenue. There is also bus service from downtown Boston and downtown Providence to Newport (America's Cup Avenue). The priory is a short cab ride from the bus station.

History: The Benedictines of Jesus Crucified was founded in 1930. The founders were convinced that poor health should not exclude women from the religious life. The congregation is of Pontifical Right.

Description: Peacefully protected by stone walls, the priory and guest house are surrounded by lawns, gardens, and tall trees.

Points of Interest: Newport abounds with sites of historic interest: the Quaker Meeting House (1699), Trinity Episcopal Church (1725), Touro Synagogue (1759), and St. Mary's Church where John F. Kennedy and Jacqueline Bouvier were wed. The Episcopal Church of S. John the Evangelist hosts British choirs every July during its annual "Celebration of English Cathedral Music." The Newport mansions and Cliff Walk are very close to the priory.

Mepkin Abbey
1098 Mepkin Abbey Road
Moncks Corner, South Carolina 29461

Telephone: (803) 761-8509. (Best time to call: 8:30 A.M. to 4:30 P.M.)

Facsimile: (803) 761-6719.

Order: Cistercian (Trappist) monks (Roman Catholic).

Accommodations: Twelve guests in the guest house in single rooms, each with private bath.

Meals: Three meals daily.

Charges: Voluntary contribution.

Write, telephone, or fax: Br. Stephen.

Directions: If driving from I-95 or from Charleston, take Route 52 to the town of Moncks Corner. From the town take Route 17A until you come to a high bridge: "The Tail Race Canal." (The bridge now also carries the name "Dennis Bishop.") A short way beyond the bridge (³⁄₁₀ mile), turn to the right on a ramp-approach onto Route 402. Follow along 402 for about two miles until you reach a public boat landing/recreation area: "Rembert Dennis." A tiny bridge is there, "Wadboo," as well as a "Mepkin Abbey" sign. As soon as you cross Wadboo Bridge, turn right immediately; you are now on Dr. Evans Road. Follow it for six miles, and you will come to the entrance of Mepkin Abbey on your right, clearly marked. Drive down the old oak-lined lane to the log Reception Center. The Guest Master will meet you when you ring the big bell.

(*Note:* Some visitors fail to turn right as they cross Wadboo Bridge. Thus, if you cross railroad tracks on Route 402, you've gone too far.)

For those using public transportation, there is Greyhound bus service to Moncks Corner, and Greyhound, Amtrak, and air services to Charleston. Please arrange in advance to be met on arrival.

History: Mepkin in an Indian word meaning "serene and lovely." From colonial times up until the early 1900s, six hundred acres here were used as a rice farm. Before the American Revolution, the patriot Henry Laurens (president of the Continental Congress) bought this land. He is buried on the property, along with other family members. In 1936 the large old plantation was purchased by Henry R. Luce, publisher/philanthropist, and his distinguished wife, the Honerable Clare Boothe Luce. Together they donated a major portion of their property to the Cistercian-Trappist monks in 1949. It was in 1993 that the abbey church was completed. The Bell Tower of the Seven Spirits is dedicated to: "The voices of all who have lived on this land: American Indians, Laurens family, African-American slaves, Luce family, friends and relatives buried here, monastic community in glory, monastic community on the way."

Description: The approach to the abbey is an impressive, broad avenue bordered by rows of ancient live oaks draped with Spanish moss. Deep in South Carolina's "Low Country," the abbey property sits along the Cooper River. Rich in varieties of flora and fauna, the beautiful old property is a place of wetlands and woodlands.

Points of Interest: Charleston, with its many historic churches, plantations, and other sites, is about an hour away.

Blue Cloud Abbey Retreat Center

Post Office Box 98
Marvin, South Dakota 57251

Telephone: (605) 432-5528.

Facsimile: (605) 432-4754.

Order: Benedictine monks (Roman Catholic).

Accommodations: Twenty guests in the monastery's guest wing, each with private bath.

Meals: Three meals daily.

Charges: Contact the Guest Master regarding charges.

Write, telephone, or fax: The Guest Master.

Directions: If driving, take US Highway 12. The abbey is thirteen miles west of Milbank, South Dakota.

For those using public transportation, there is air transportation to Watertown, South Dakota, and bus service to Milbank. Contact the Guest Master for further directions.

History: Benedictine monks from St. Meinrad Archabbey, Indiana, arrived in the Dakotas in 1876 with the dream of founding a monastery among Native Americans. It was not until 1954 that the dream became a reality, when missionaries of the Dakotas' four reservations united to found what in time became Blue Cloud Abbey. The namesake of the abbey is an American Indian. A Christian, he persevered in his faith despite the infrequent visits of passing missionaries. Today the abbey is home to about forty monks, some of whom staff parishes in the Dakotas, while others live at the abbey and pursue prayer, study, farming, printing, the design and manufacture of ecclesiastical vestments, and the ministry of hospitality.

Description: Overlooking the vast Whetstone Valley of the Glacial Lakes Region of northeastern South Dakota, the abbey sits on a hill and occupies buildings built by the monks themselves.

Points of Interest: Historic Fort Sisseton, the Sisseton/Wahpeton Indian Reservation, and many lakes are located in this region of "The Sunshine State."

St. Mary's Retreat and Conference Center

Post Office Box 188
Sewanee, Tennessee 37375

Telephone: (615) 598-5342. (Best time to call: Monday through Friday 8:00 A.M. to 4:00 P.M.)

Facsimile: (615) 598-5884.

Order: Affiliated with the Community of St. Mary (Episcopal).

Accommodations: Forty-four guests in several kinds of rooms: single, double suites, and a hermitage (private cabin). Four apartments (suites) have private baths; the rest have shared baths.

Meals: Three meals daily.

Charges: $18.50 to $35.00 per person per day for room. Breakfast is $6.00, lunch is $7.50, and dinner is $8.50.

Write, telephone, or fax: Clara Stephens, Director.

Directions: If driving from Nashville or Chattanooga, take I-24 and exit at the Monteagle/Sewanee exit. Turn toward the University of the South or Sewanee on Highway 41A. You will pass the State Highway 156 turnoff at St. Andrews, the University of the South turnoff, Sewanee Pharmacy, and Sewanee Market. Continue past all of these until you reach State Highway 56, then turn left toward Sherwood. Proceed about one mile on Highway 56 to the first major bend in the road to the left and turn directly right, onto St. Mary's Lane. This turn is marked with an "Episcopal Church Welcomes You" sign. Drive through the stone pillars with a cross on the left. Continue on this road until you reach the gravel parking area on the right. The office is inside the door with the sign "St. Mary's Episcopal Center."

There is no public transportation.

Description: St. Mary's is set high atop Tennessee's Cumberland Plateau, and guests may enjoy spectacular scenery from the windows of their rooms or anywhere on the ruggedly beautiful property. Visitors may wish to explore the miles of trails on the two-hundred-acre facility, which includes a pond, forests, rocky slopes and, in season, fields of wildflowers. This is a secluded place of cool, green summers and vibrant autumn color, "a place made for reflection, renewal, relaxation and thought…"

Points of Interest: Just two miles down the road is the University of the South with its awe-inspiring Gothic Revival chapel. Also in the area are seven state natural areas, state parks (including Tims Ford), and other places of interest, such as Hundred Oaks Castle, the Cowan Railroad Museum, Falls Mill, and the Old Jail Museum.

Monastery of the Four Evangelists

3011 Roe Drive
Houston, Texas 77087-2409

Telephone: (713) 645-0843. (Best time to call: Monday through Friday 10:00 A.M. to 4:00 P.M.)

Facsimile: (713) 645-0104.

Order: Monks (Ukrainian Autocephalous Orthodox Church).

Accommodations: Twenty-eight men in twenty-one guest rooms and seven guest cells, all with shared baths. There is also one hermitage with private bath.

Meals: Three meals daily.

Charges: $15 for room and $10 for meals per person per day.

Write, telephone, or fax: The Guest Master.

Directions: Contact the Guest Master for directions by car and by public transportation.

History: The monastery was founded on Palm Sunday, 1976, "as an inner-city monastic presence witnessing to the principle that the great urban centers of our country are the spiritual deserts of the twentieth century." The initial facilities were very basic, if that, and the poverty of the monks real. Through prayer, hard work, inciteful planning, and the generosity of benefactors, the monastery has grown in members and physical plant.

Description: Today the monastery has two chapels: that used by the monks, which is filled with many handmade icons and several historical appurtenances, and an ecumenical chapel "inspired by the presence of a mosque within the walls of St. Catherine's monastery on Mt. Sinai, Egypt," where those of other faiths may hold services. There is also a site for a future cathedral here. Guests may lodge in Cathedral Manor or in one of the cells in the "kellia." St. Paisij Hermitage is a small air-conditioned cottage with private bath and a kitchenette for long-term retreatants.

The monastic brotherhood is engaged in many works, including a press, the Eastern Orthodox Choral Society, the Institute for Eastern Orthodox Studies, Orthodox Charities, and the Cathedral Parish of St. John Chrysostom, "ministering to the spiritual needs of English- and Spanish-speaking converts, ethnic Ukrainians and Belarusians, and Old Kalendarists of every ethnic group."

Points of Interest: Houston, the largest city in Texas, is home to Rice and other universities, the Johnson Space Center, and the Astrodome. Just north of the city is the George Bush Presidential Library in Bryan College Station.

Mount Carmel Center

4600 West Davis Street
Dallas, Texas 75211-3498

Telephone: (214) 331-6224.

Facsimile: (214) 330-0844.

Order: Discalced Carmelite friars (Roman Catholic).

Accommodations: Up to eighteen guests (all men or all women) in single and double rooms, one of which has a private bath.

Meals: One cooked meal is served most days; refrigerated foods are available for other meals.

Charges: $30 per person per night.

Write, telephone, or fax: The Guest Master.

Directions: Contact the Guest Master for directions by car and by public transportation.

History: The Discalced Carmelites began as a reform in sixteenth-century Spain, led by St. Teresa of Avila and St. John of the Cross. Mount Carmel Center, primarily a monastery for Carmelite friars, also serves as an informal institute of Christian spirituality. The center was opened in 1974.

Description: Mount Carmel Center, on thirty acres atop a hill, overlooks Dallas and the surrounding countryside. Guests may walk on the wooded grounds and use the large contemporary chapel as well as the smaller Byzantine oratory.

Points of Interest: Reunion Tower offers views for miles in all directions. The Texas School Book Depository building is open to the public, and the city's monument to President Kennedy is at John F. Kennedy Plaza. Old City Park is a museum of living history, where turn-of-the-century churches, homes, and other buildings may be visited.

Special Note: Please contact the Center for information on special programs and liturgical celebrations.

Abbey of Our Lady of the Holy Trinity

1250 South 9500 East
Huntsville, Utah 84317

Telephone: (801) 745-3784 or (801) 745-3931. (Best times to call: 8:00 A.M. to 12:00 noon and 2:30 P.M. to 5:00 P.M.)

Facsimile: (801) 745-6430.

Order: Cistercian (Trappist) monks (Roman Catholic).

Accommodations: Twelve men in the monastery in single rooms, all with shared bath.

Meals: Three meals daily.

Charges: Voluntary offering.

Write, telephone, or fax: The Guest Master.

Directions: If driving from Salt Lake City (south) or from points north, take Interstate 15 to Ogden. Then take Route 39 east toward Huntsville. On Route 39, just before Huntsville and after the Texaco gas station on your right, make a right turn at the monastery sign.

For those using public transportation, there is air service to Salt Lake City Airport (fifty miles away). From the city and airport there is bus service to Huntsville's post office. Please call or arrange in advance for pickup.

History: Originating in France in the twelfth century, the Order of Cistercians of Strict Observance (the Trappists) have been in North America since 1848. Nearly a century later, in 1947, Trappist monks settled in the Ogden Valley, an area "well suited to our needs for seclusion and beauty." Today the Utah community numbers about twenty-five monks.

Description: Unique in the history of monastic architecture, Trinity Abbey is composed of a quadrangle of Quonset buildings, which the monks find "functional and adequate." Their farm includes 750 acres of irrigated fields that produce barley, alfalfa, and wheat. The wheat is used in the monks' bakery to bake their whole wheat and raisin breads. The farm also has a poultry department and about three hundred beef cattle from which the monks sell calves and steers. Beyond the farm, the abbey includes 1,100 acres of hill rangeland.

Special Note: The monks produce creamed honey and liquid honey, which they sell by mail order.

Monastery of the Immaculate Heart of Mary

H.C.R. #13, Box 11
Westfield, Vermont 05874

Telephone: (802) 744-6525. (Best times to call: 11:00 A.M. to 12:00 noon and 3:00 P.M. to 5:00 P.M.)

Order: Benedictine nuns (Roman Catholic).

Accommodations: Three women in the guest house, each in a single room, and all with shared baths.

Meals: Three meals daily.

Charges: $30 per person per day for room and meals.

Write or telephone: The Guest Mistress.

Directions: If driving on I-89 or I-91, take Route 100 to Westfield.

For those using public transportation, there is air service to Burlington (two hours away) and bus service to Newport, Vermont (thirty minutes away). From either arrival point, taxi or car rental service is available to the monastery.

History: The Benedictine monastery of the Immaculate Heart of Mary has its roots in the eleventh-century abbey of Saint-Pierre de Solesmes, France. It was the great liturgist Dom Gueranger who restored monastic life to the monastery at Solesmes after the French Revolution. From there stemmed the Congregation of Solesmes—a part of the Benedictine family—which today has eight monasteries of nuns and twenty-one of monks in Europe, Africa, and the Americas. It was in 1981 that nuns from the Abbaye Sainte-Marie des Deux-Montagnes (Canada) founded the Westfield monastery.

Description: Westfield is located in the beautiful "Northeast Kingdom" corner of Vermont. Here one is surrounded by open fields, pine forests, deciduous trees, birds, deer, and other animals. The red brick monastery, with its traditional monastic building floor plan, is attractively designed with pitched roofs, bell towers, and windows that overlook scenes of nature's beauty. This setting reflects the traditional vocation, attire, and life-style of the nuns, who sing Latin Gregorian chant at services in their chapel. Seven times a day and once at night the tower bell calls the nuns to the monastery church to "sing the praise of the Lord."

Weston Priory
Weston, Vermont 05161

Telephone: (802) 824-5409.

Order: Benedictine monks (Roman Catholic).

Accommodations: Six men in St. Gabriel's Guest House, each in a single room and all with shared baths. There are accommodations for five women in Morningside Guest House, each in a single room and all with shared bath. (In addition, there are accommodations for a group of up to eight adults in Bethany House and for a group of up to five adults in Romero House.)

Meals: Individual guests have three meals daily with the brothers. Groups are requested to bring their own food and to prepare their meals in the kitchen of their guest house.

Charges: Freewill offering.

Write or telephone: The Guest Brother.

Directions: If driving, take I-91 to Exit 6, then Route 103 west to Chester. Continue west on Route 11 and make a right at Hetty-Green's Motel. When you get to Weston village, make a right onto Route 100 and continue north for four miles to the junction of Route 155. Weston Priory is on the first road to the left north on Route 155.

Contact the Guest Brother for directions by public transportation.

History: A monk of Dormition Abbey in Jerusalem, Abbot Leo Rudloff, founded Weston Priory in 1953.

Description: The simple, rustic monastery, chapel, guest houses, and other buildings are located on the edge of the Green Mountain National Forest. The monks of Weston have become widely known for their music and crafts. Albums, cassettes, songbooks, and crafts are sold at the priory.

Points of Interest: Often called the prettiest village in Vermont, Weston is on the National Register of Historic Places. The Weston Playhouse is the oldest professional summer theater in Vermont. The Old Parish Church (1803) and the Church on the Hill are fine examples of nineteenth-century rural New England ecclesiastical architecture.

Special Note: The ordinary length of stay at the priory guest houses is from three days to one week. Reservations should be made at least four to six months in advance. Maps, brochures, and further information are available from the priory's Guest Brother.

Mary Mother of the Church Abbey

Benedictine Retreat/Conference Facilities
12617 River Road
Richmond, Virginia 23233-6139

Telephone: (804) 784-3508, ext. 225. (Best time to call: 9:00 A.M. to 4:00 P.M.)

Facsimile: (804) 784-3508, ext. 245.

Order: Benedictine monks (Roman Catholic).

Accommodations: Fifty-four guests in the monastery guest wing in single and double rooms, some with private baths.

Meals: Three meals daily.

Charges: $35 per person per night, single occupancy, and $30 per person per night, double occupancy. Breakfast is $5, lunch is $6, and dinner is $8.

Write, telephone, or fax: Brother Matthew E. Miller, O.S.B., Guest Master.

Directions: For those using public transportation, there are air, bus, and Amtrak services to Richmond. Contact the Guest Master for further directions.

History: Founded in 1911, this community became an independent abbey in 1989. Today the abbey is home to nearly twenty monks who pursue the Benedictine ideal of *Ora et Labora* (Work and Prayer) at the abbey, in their parish and high school, and through chaplaincies.

Description: Protected by a field on one side and the historic James River on the other, the abbey is a rambling modern structure. At its center is the circular abbey church where the monks gather four times daily for services.

Points of Interest: Colonial Williamsburg is sixty miles south of Richmond. En route are antebellum plantations that sit on the shores of the James River, as does the abbey. The area also has a number of colonial Anglican churches worth visiting. The history of Richmond, the state capital and one-time Confederate capital, is displayed in the Valentine Museum. Among other sites, guests may visit the Museum and White House of the Confederacy and the Richmond National Battlefield Park.

Our Lady of the Angels Monastery

3365 Monastery Drive
Crozet, Virginia 22932

Telephone: (804) 823-1452. (Best times to call: 9:00 A.M. to 11:00 A.M. and 2:00 P.M. to 4:00 P.M.)

Facsimile: (804) 823-6379.

Order: Cistercian (Trappistine) nuns (Roman Catholic).

Accommodations: Up to ten guests in two log cabin cottages, each with shared bath.

Meals: None. Guests self-prepare meals using the kitchen facilities in each cottage.

Charges: Donations.

Write, telephone, or fax: Sister Barbara.

Directions: If driving on I-81, exit onto I-64 east, then stay on 64 east until Exit 107 (exit to Route 250). At the end of the exit ramp, go left onto Route 250 going east. After about one mile this intersects with Route 240 at a blinking light. Turn left onto Route 240 (going north now) and continue on right through the little town of Crozet. In the middle of Crozet, Route 240 makes a 90-degree turn to the right and goes east to Charlottesville. *Do not make this right turn but continue straight ahead.* At this point the road in front of you is Route 810; stay on this until it ends four miles beyond Crozet, at the tiny township of White Hall. Route 810 dead-ends here into Route 614 (also called Garth Road). Turn right onto Route 614 (Garth Road) and go east on it for two miles; then turn left onto Millington Road and go north on it for one mile. At the end of that mile you will go over a bridge. Just thirty feet beyond this bridge is the actual road to the monastery—Clark Road (also marked Route 674). Turn left onto Clark Road; this is a very winding, narrow gravel lane, so you'll need to drive slowly. After about one mile you will see the monastery, a large brick building, up on the hill to your right. The driveway is clearly marked "Our Lady of the Angels Monastery," and you can follow it all the way up to the building and park just outside the front door. Ring the doorbell outside and then come in.

If driving from points northeast, take Route 29 to Charlottesville. At the intersection of Route 29 and Barracks Road (a major intersection in Charlottesville), go west on Barracks Road away from the city. Out in the country Barracks Road becomes Garth Road (also Route 614), but it is obviously the same road. Your first turnoff will be approximately nine-and-one-half miles from the intersection of Route 29 and Barracks Road. This is Millington Road (also marked Route 671), which comes in on the right only. Continue as directed above.

For those using public transportation, there are air, bus, and train services to Charlottesville. Contact Sister Barbara for further directions.

History: The monastery's cornerstone concisely tells its history:

> May 1, 1987
> Our Lady of the Angels Monastery
> Founded by faith, love and sacrifice
> of Mt. St. Mary's Abbey
> Wrentham, Massachusetts

Description: Set in the foothills of the Blue Ridge Mountains, the red brick monastery is surrounded by rolling fields and woodlands. One of the guest log cabins, across the way from the monastery, dates to 1810.

Points of Interest: Just a few miles east of Crozet is Charlottesville. There one may visit Monticello (home of Thomas Jefferson), Ash Lawn (home of James Monroe), and the University of Virginia's 1819 Rotunda. West of Crozet are the Skyline Drive and the Blue Ridge Parkway.

Special Note: The log cabins are open to guests from April through November.

The nuns support themselves through the manufacture and sale of Gouda cheese, which may be purchased at the monastery or through mail order.

Convent of St. Helena

1114 21st Avenue East
Seattle, Washington 98112-3513

Telephone: (206) 325-2830.

Facsimile: (206) 325-0405.

Order: Order of St. Helena (Episcopal).

Accommodations: Eight guests in the convent in four twin-bedded rooms, all with shared bath.

Meals: Two meals daily.

Charges: Freewill offering accepted, but suggested amounts for room and meals are $35 per day for a single room, or $45 per day for a twin-bedded room.

Write, telephone, or fax: A Sister.

Directions: If driving, exit from I-5 onto East Madison Street, going east. Turn left onto 19th Avenue East. Pass two four-way stop signs with red blinkers. At the next street, turn right (east) on East Prospect Street, then left onto 21st Avenue East. The convent is the second house on the right.

If using public transportation from downtown Seattle, take Metro bus 12, labeled for Interlaken Park. (This bus can be boarded at 1st Avenue at Union or on Marion Street.) Get off at 19th Avenue East and East Prospect Street. Walk two blocks east to 21st Avenue East. Turn left. The convent is the second house on the right.

Metro bus 43 is another option. Get off the bus at 23rd Avenue East at East Aloha Street. Walk two blocks west on Aloha and then one block north on 21st Street. Cross Prospect. The convent is the second house on the right.

History: The newest foundation of the Order of St. Helena, the convent was opened in 1983.

Description: The convent is a large private house in the Capital Hill district of Seattle. The house is "Seattle Tudor" in style and was built around 1910 in a residential area of similar homes.

Points of Interest: Seattle is located on the Puget Sound, with the Cascade Mountains to the east and the Olympic Mountains to the west. Mount Rainier is visible from many parts of the city. Seattle's Metro bus system provides easy access to sights in and near the city. There are two parks within walking distance of the convent.

Special Note: A schedule of events is available from the Guest Sister.

St. Martin's Abbey Guest House

5300 Pacific Avenue S.E.
Lacey, Washington 98503

Telephone: (206) 438-4457.

Order: Benedictine monks (Roman Catholic).

Accommodations: Eighteen guests in ten rooms (two single and eight twin). Each room has a sink and shared bath down the corridor.

Meals: Three meals daily.

Charges: $25 per person per day for room and meals.

Write or telephone: The Guest Master, Br. Edmund, O.S.B.

Directions: By car from Seattle, take I-5 about sixty miles south to Lacey. Take Exit 109.

There is air service to Seattle-Tacoma Airport (about one hour north of Lacey). Amtrak and Greyhound have services to Olympia (about two miles south of Lacey.)

History: When Benedictine monks arrived in Washington in 1895, the Pacific Northwest was still a pioneer region. From its inception, education was a priority at St. Martin's, and today its monks administer and teach at the coeducational St. Martin's College.

Description: The guest house and campus share an attractive, peaceful, and tranquil setting. The abbey church was completed in 1971. Its warm wooden interior, rich with symbolism and art, is designed for a flexible use of space and has become the model for a number of churches of various denominations.

Points of Interest: The Pacific Northwest is heavily wooded with tall fir, cedar, hemlock, and other species of trees. The Pacific Ocean is a forty-five minute drive west of the abbey, and the historic sights of Seattle are one hour's drive north. The majestic Mount Rainier can be seen for many miles and from many directions.

Special Note: A brochure describing the guest house is available from the abbey's Guest Master. Groups are welcome at the abbey but must provide their own retreat director.

Good Counsel Friary

Route 7, Box 183
Tyrone Road
Morgantown, West Virginia 26505-9199

Telephone: (304) 594-1714. (Best times to call: Tuesday and Thursday, 9:00 A.M. to 4:00 P.M.; Monday, Wednesday, and Friday, 9:00 A.M. to 10:30 A.M.)

Facsimile: (304) 594-9247.

Order: Franciscan Friars (Roman Catholic).

Accommodations: Thirty-nine guests in thirteen triple-occupancy rooms, all with shared baths.

Meals: Three meals daily (except Tuesday supper).

Charges: Donation.

Write, telephone, or fax: The Father Superior.

Directions: If driving from points south, follow Interstate 79 north and get off at Exit 148 for Interstate 68 east in the direction of Cumberland, Maryland. Get off at Exit 7 and make a right onto Route 857 north. Go two miles to Tyrone Road (*not* Tyrone/ Avery). Make a right onto Tyrone Road and the friary is 1.3 miles up on the left.

If driving from points east, take Interstate 68 west from Cumberland, Maryland. Get off at Exit 10 in West Virginia for Route 857 and make a right. Go about 500 feet, then make a left on Route 857 south. Pass Lakeview Resort on the left, cross the old Cheat Lake Bridge; Tyrone Road is the first left after the bridge. The friary is on Tyrone Road 1.3 miles up on the left. Alternately, take Route 7 west past Kingwood and Masontown, West Virginia. After passing Greer Limestone, at Pioneer Rocks, make a right onto Tyrone Road. The friary is 3.1 miles up on the right.

From the west, get on Interstate 70 east out of Washington, Pennsylvania, and follow signs for Interstate 79 south in the direction of Waynesburg, Pennsylvania. Get off at Exit 148 for Interstate 68 east in the direction of Waynesburg, Pennsylvania. Get off at Exit 148 for Interstate 68 east in the direction of Cumberland, Maryland. Get off at Exit 7 and make a right onto Route 857 north. Go two miles to Tyrone Road (*not* Tyrone/Avery). Make a right onto Tyrone Road and the friary is 1.3 miles up on the left.

From Morgantown, follow Route 119 north, pass the airport, and pick up Route 857 north and follow it all they way to Tyrone Road. Then make a right onto Tyrone Road (*not* Tyrone/Avery); the friary is 1.3 miles up on the left.

From Evansdale, take 705 east to the end. Make a left onto Route 119 north and follow above directions to Morgantown.

From the North, follow Interstate 79 south in the direction of Washington, Pennsylvania, and Waynesburg, Pennsylvania. Get off at Exit 148 for Interstate 68 east in the direction of Cumberland, Maryland. Get off at Exit 7 and make a right onto Route 857 north. Go two miles to Tyrone Road (*not* Tyrone/Avery); make a right onto Tyrone Road. The friary is 1.3 miles up on the left. Alternately, follow Route 51 south to

212

Uniontown, Pennsylvania; take 119 south bypass to Route 43 south. At the end, make a left to get on 857. At the stop sign, make a right onto 857 south and take all the way to West Virginia. Pass Bruceton Bank and bear to the right; pass Lakeview Resort and cross the old Cheat Lake Bridge. Tyrone Road is the first left after the bridge. The friary is on Tyrone Road 1.3 miles up on the left. Another alternative is to take 119 south toward Connellsville and Uniontown, Pennsylvania, and follow the above directions for 119 south to the friary. Yet another alternative is to take 119 south out of Masontown, Pennsylvania, and Pt. Marion, Pennsylvania, and when you come to 857, stay straight on 857 north. Pass the entrance for Interstate 68, continue for two miles to Tyrone Road, then make a right onto Tyrone Road (*not* Tyrone/Avery); the friary is 1.3 miles up on the left.

For those using public transportation, there are air and Greyhound bus services to Morgantown. Contact Fr. Superior for further directions.

History: It was the beloved St. Francis who founded the Order of Friars Minor in thirteenth-century Assisi, Italy. The friars, popularly known as "Franciscans" arrived in the Americas as early as the sixteenth century.

Description: The friary, just seven miles east of Morgantown, is set on fifteen well-manicured acres. Most noteworthy is the twenty-three-room stone "castle," built on the property in 1933. Other buildings include the chapel, a large three-story friary and renewal center. For recreation there are a football field, a volleyball court, a basketball court, horseshoe pits, and a picnic area.

Points of Interest: West Virginia is appropriately nicknamed "The Mountain State," and visitors will be impressed by the natural beauty of this area.

Convent of the Holy Nativity

101 East Division Street
Fond du Lac, Wisconsin 54935

Telephone: (414) 921-2560.

Order: Sisters of the Holy Nativity (Episcopal).

Accommodations: Twenty-seven guests in the convent in single rooms, all with shared bath.

Meals: Three meals daily.

Charges: $20 per person per day for room and meals.

Write or telephone: The Guest Sister.

Directions: Contact the convent's Guest Sister for directions.

History: The Sisterhood of the Holy Nativity was begun in Boston in 1882 by Charles Chapman Grafton, a priest of the Episcopal Church. When he was consecrated bishop of Fond du Lac, the sisters followed Bishop Grafton to Wisconsin, there establishing the Convent of the Holy Nativity.

Description: The Gothic Revival convent, built at the turn of the century, has an exceptionally beautiful chapel, its interior fitted with fine wood carving. In the spirit of the founder, the sisters "open their chapels generously for retreats and private devotions of the devout-minded, whether Associates of the Sisterhood or not."

Points of Interest: Fond du Lac has long been a center for the Anglo-Catholic movement in the Episcopal Church. The city's Cathedral Church of St. Paul is listed on the National Register of Historic Places.

Special Note: Group retreats are offered several times a year at the convent. Descriptive brochures and further information may be obtained from the convent's Guest Sister.

Holy Hill
1525 Carmel Road
Hubertus, Wisconsin 53033

Telephone: (414) 628-1838. (Best time to call: Monday through Friday 8:00 A.M. to 4:00 P.M.)

Order: Discalced Carmelite Friars (Roman Catholic).

Accommodations: Twenty-eight guests in the guest house in twin-bedded rooms, each with private bath.

Meals: Available in the cafeteria.

Charges: $26 per room per night, single occupancy, and $40 per room per night, double occupancy, plus tax.

Write or telephone: The monastery office.

Directions: If driving from Chicago, take Interstate 94 north toward Milwaukee. From Milwaukee, take Highway 41 north to Highway 167, then continue west to Holy Hill.

There is no public transportation available.

History: The Carmelites were founded in spirit by the Prophet Elias on Mount Carmel in the Holy Land. The order grew in numbers throughout medieval Europe, and it was the Spanish mystic and Doctor of the Church St. Theresa of Avila who reformed parts of the order in the sixteenth century. As a badge of their reform, her followers wore sandals and were nicknamed "barefoot" (or discalced) Carmelites. A group of German Discalced Carmelite friars resettled in Wisconsin, there establishing Holy Hill.

Description: Listed on the National Register of Historic Places, Holy Hill is crowned by a massive Romanesque Revival church, complete with mosaics and priceless German stained-glass windows. This is the National Shrine of Our Lady Help of Christians. Guests can visit the outdoor Stations of the Cross, the Lourdes grotto, or more secluded spots on the four-hundred-acre shrine property, which is crossed by Wisconsin's Ice Age Trail. There is a flight of 178 steps leading to the top of the church's spire. Those who venture up are rewarded with unrivaled panoramas of the surrounding countryside and the Milwaukee skyline on the horizon.

Mary's Margin
S83 W27815 Beaver Trail
Mukwonago, Wisconsin 53149

Telephone: (414) 363-8489. (Best time to call: 7:00 P.M. to 9:00 P.M.)

Order: Sisters of St. Mary (Episcopal).

Accommodations: Up to four guests in one room with two double beds and one private bath.

Meals: Three meals daily (vegetarian).

Charges: Donations. In addition, guests are often assigned an hour of manual labor each day, such as housework, gathering/carrying/ stacking firewood, yard work, or snow shoveling.

Write or telephone: The Guest Mistress.

Directions: If driving from Milwaukee, take Highway 43 south. Make a right onto Highway 164, then a left on "ES" and a right on Hillview (this will be the second right after "XX"). Then make a left on Whitetail and a right on Beaver Trail to the driveway at the end of the road.

If driving from points north or south, take Highway 83, east on "ES" in Mukwonago and left on Hillview (which is the third left after crossing the Fox River). Then make a left on Whitetail as directed above.

If using public transportation, contact the Guest Mistress for directions.

History: The Community of St. Mary, the oldest religious community in the Episcopal Church, was founded in New York City in 1865. It was in 1904 that the Western Province, based in Wisconsin, was begun and set apart. Today the sisters of the Western Province "live singly or in small groups, each sister using her gifts for ministry as she feels led with support and blessing from the whole group." They "try to foster and maintain a simple and healthy life-style, shared with… guests, a regard for the natural world around us, a concern for justice and peace for all people, and a desire to grow through study and reflection."

Description: Set on four acres in beautifully wooded hills overlooking the Fox River Valley, Mary's Margin has an enchanting little chapel. The house includes a spacious and comfortable great room, which overlooks a picturesque marsh.

Special Note: On many Saturday evenings the sisters have a two-hour "Sabbath Vigil" consisting of readings, psalms, danced chants or hymns, and periods of silence.

San Benito Monastery

859 Main Street
Post Office Box 520
Dayton, Wyoming 82836

Telephone: (307) 655-9013. (Best times to call: 9:00 A.M. to 12:00 noon and 2:00 P.M. to 5:00 P.M.)

Facsimile: (307) 655-9052.

Order: Benedictine sisters of Perpetual Adoration (Roman Catholic).

Accommodations: Six guests in two mobile homes, each with three bedrooms, living room, kitchen/dining room combination, and bath.

Meals: Three meals daily.

Charges: $25 per person per night.

Write, telephone, or fax: The Guest Mistress.

Directions: If driving from Sheridan, Wyoming, take Highway 90 north. Pick up Highway 14 and continue through Ranchester to Dayton. Drive through town; on the way out, going toward the mountains, there will be a small blue sign at the end of a small bridge with the monastery house number: 589. Turn left on that road. The monastery, a cluster of blue buildings, is at the end of the road.

For those using public transportation, United Airlines has service to Sheridan. Contact the Guest Mistress for pickup on arrival.

History: The Benedictine Sisters of Perpetual Adoration have their roots in the rolling hills of northwest Missouri. There, in the town of Clyde, the community had its beginning in 1882. Today the sisters have a number of independent monasteries, all west of the Mississippi River. Their newest foundation, San Benito Monastery, was opened in 1983. Here the community welcomes guests with the Benedictine spirit of hospitality and helps to support itself through the baking and sale of altar breads.

Description: San Benito Monastery is a village of blue houses on thirty-eight acres of woodland and cleared fields. The Big Horn Mountains can clearly be seen from San Benito.

Points of Interest: Dayton is home to some of the largest cattle ranches in the world. On many summer weekends there are cowboy roping events in the area. This corner of Wyoming, "The Equality State," is filled with historic sites, Indian culture, and cowboy folklore. From the monastery it is a twenty-minute drive to the top of the Big Horn Mountains and less than that to the beautiful Tongue River Canyon. Yellowstone National Park is about a five-hour drive from Dayton.

Canada

St. John's Priory

11717 93rd Street
Edmonton, Alberta T5G 1E2

Telephone: (403) 474-7465. (Best times to call: 10:10 A.M. to 11:30 A.M., 2:00 P.M. to 4:45 P.M., and 6:30 P.M. to 7:00 P.M.)

Facsimile: (403) 479-6280.

Order: Sisterhood of St. John the Divine (Anglican Church of Canada).

Accommodations: Four women and three men in the priory, each in a single room and all with shared baths.

Meals: Three meals daily.

Charges: $25 for room and $5 for meals per person per day.

Write, telephone, or fax: The Guest Sister.

Directions: The priory is located in the city of Edmonton near the U.S. Stadium and the Coliseum.

For those using public transportation, buses numbers 5 and 18 go by the priory. Contact the Guest Sister for more detailed directions.

History: The Sisterhood of St. John the Divine, founded in Toronto in 1884, has been ministering in the Anglican Diocese of Edmonton since the 1930s.

Description: The priory includes a chapel with a bright, contemporary tapestry behind its freestanding altar, a library, an invitingly peaceful garden, and a book room where books, posters, and cards may be bought.

Points of Interest: Edmonton's Provincial Museum contains exhibits featuring the area's natural history and ethnology. Fort Edmonton Park, set in a ravine of the Saskatchewan River, is a historic re-creation of the European settlement of the city. Farther up the river is Muttart Conservatory, its pyramid/greenhouses displaying plants from various climatic zones. The Legislative Building (1912) and Art Gallery are also downtown. The observatory known as Vista 33 provides panoramic views of the city and surrounding areas.

Special Note: "We have pets—poodles and cats."

The Prince of Peace Priory

Post Office Box 960
Chemainus, British Columbia V0R 1K0

Telephone: (604) 246-9578.

Order: Order of Agape and Reconciliation (ecumenical).

Accommodations: Four guests in one twin and two single rooms in St. Mary's House of Prayer and in St. Bede's House, some with private bath.

Meals: Three meals daily.

Charges: $30 per person per day for room and meals.

Write or telephone: The Guest Master.

Directions: If driving from Victoria, take Highway 1 north. The drive will be about one-and-one-quarter hours.

For those using public transportation, there is bus service from Victoria to Nanaimo and ferry service from Tsawassen or Horseshoe Bay to Nanaimo. Please contact the priory for further directions.

History: The Order of Agape and Reconciliation, founded in 1972, is built on the tradition of Little Gidding (a seventeenth-century community in the Church of England). Members include men and women, and married and single. Begun under Anglican auspices, the order is ecumenical in outreach and includes Roman Catholics, Protestants, and Eastern Orthodox among its members in fourteen countries. The Prince of Peace Priory was dedicated in 1987.

Description: The Chapel of St. Nicholas of Flue and other buildings are located in a quiet and peaceful rural area with fields and forests.

Points of Interest: The priory is on Vancouver Island. Victoria—the capital of British Columbia—is a beautiful city on the southeast corner of the island. Pacific Rim National Park is on the west coast.

Special Note: In addition to receiving individual guests, the priory offers Ignatian retreats. Advance inquiry and advance reservations are required for these. For more information (and reference requirements), please contact Father Cyril, O.A.R.

Our Lady of the Prairies Abbey

Post Office Box 310
Holland, Manitoba R0G 0X0

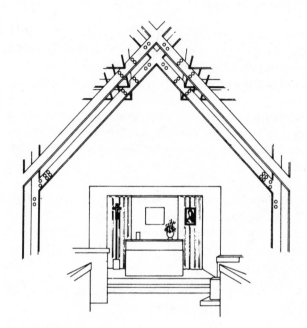

Telephone: (204) 526-2000.

Order: Cistercian (Trappist) monks (Roman Catholic).

Accommodations: Eight guests: four in the monastery in single rooms with private baths, and four in the guest house in single rooms with shared baths.

Meals: Three meals daily.

Charges: $25 per person per day for room and meals. Contact the Guest Master for more information.

Write or telephone: Brother Andre, O.C.S.O., Guest Master.

Directions: If driving from Winnipeg, take Route 2 west to Holland, a two-hour drive.

For those using public transportation, there is air service to Winnipeg. Contact the Guest Master for more information and directions.

History: The Abbey of Bellefontaine, France, founded Notre-Dame des Prairies in 1892. Initially located in St. Norbert, a suburb of Winnipeg, the monastery transferred to Holland in 1978 "in order to regain the solitude necessary to monastic life."

Description: The abbey is in an agricultural setting surrounded by rolling hills and clusters of tall, old trees. Occasionally groups of deer may be seen grazing not far from the monastery and guest house.

Points of Interest: Spruce Woods Park is near the abbey. The Manitoba Agricultural Museum, with its collections of giant antique tractors and threshing machines, is nearby in the town of Austin.

Trappistines, Abbaye Notre-Dame de l'Assomption

Rogersville, New Brunswick E0A 2T0

Telephone: (506) 775-2322.

Facsimile: (506) 775-6295.

Order: Cistercian (Trappistine) nuns (Roman Catholic).

Accommodations: Seven women in the guest wing of the monastery in single rooms, all with shared baths.

Meals: Three meals daily.

Charges: Suggested donation of $25 per person per day for room and meals.

Write, telephone, or fax: The Guest Mistress.

Directions: If driving, take the Trans Canada Highway to Route 26 (from Moncton going toward Miramichi).

For those using public transportation, VIA Rail (on its route between Halifax and Montreal) stops in Rogersville. Please contact the Guest Mistress for additional information and directions.

History: The Cistercian nuns date back to twelfth-century France. This particular community was founded in Lyons, France, in 1820, transferred to Canada in 1904, and was raised to the status of an abbey in 1927.

Description: The abbey church, monastery, barns, and other buildings are in the midst of farm fields and forests of pine and birch trees. The nuns provide for their basic needs through farming. Additional support is earned through the sale of their altar breads. This is a bilingual community (French and English) whose liturgy is in French.

The Recluse Sisters

Box 51431, SS #3
St. John's, Newfoundland A1B 4M2

Telephone: (709) 437-1243.

Facsimile: (709) 437-1243.

Order: The Recluse Sisters (Roman Catholic).

Accommodations: Two guests, each in a single room, with shared bath.

Meals: Guests are provided with a kitchenette with microwave oven.

Charges: There is a suggested fee of $25 per person per day.

Write, telephone, or fax: The Guest Mistress.

Directions: If driving, take a ferry from Nova Scotia to Channel-Port aux Basques, Newfoundland. From there take the Trans-Canada Highway to St. John's.

If using public transportation, take a ferry to Channel-Port aux Basques, a bus to St. John's, and then a taxi to the convent.

History: Though a relatively young religious community, the Recluse Sisters were founded in spirit more than three centuries ago by Jeanne LeBer (1662–1714). She chose to live her life in prayerful solitude, first in her family's house in Ville Marie (now Montreal) and later as a solitary recluse in a small room attached to a convent chapel. She remained in strict seclusion for thirty-four years until her death at the age of fifty-two. Inspired by her, the Recluse Sisters, a contemplative institute, was founded in 1943. In 1989 the Newfoundland convent was established in response to the invitation of the local archbishop.

Description: The Recluse Sisters occupy a lovely house in Outer Cove. With pitched roofs, dormers, and bay windows, the convent is surrounded by lawns and trees. Guests have access to the chapel and a library of books and audiotapes. It is but a twenty-minute walk from the convent to Outer Cove's seashore.

Points of Interest: "Ruggedly beautiful" is an apt way to describe Newfoundland's 6,000-mile-long coastline. Deep fjords, towering cliffs, coves, and bays mark the coastline of "The Rock," as the province is nicknamed. Inland are lakes, rivers, and dense forests. In the city of St. John's, visitors may climb to the top of the Cabot Tower on Signal Hill for outstanding views of the city and coastline. The Old City has two particularly noteworthy historic churches: the twin-towered Roman Catholic basilica (1850), built on the highest point in the city, and the stone Gothic Revival Anglican cathedral (1843), both of which share the city's namesake and patron—St. John the Baptist.

Special Note: The sisters offer "accommodations in the guest facilities of the monastery for anyone seeking a propitious place to meet the Lord in prayer, silence, and peace."

Through Him, with Him, in Him

—The Sisters' motto

Nova Nada

Kemptville, Yarmouth Co.
Nova Scotia B0W 1Y0

Telephone: None

Order: Spiritual Life Institute Community (Roman Catholic).

Accommodations: Five guests in separate hermitages, most with a private bath.

Meals: There are two communal meals weekly. The hermitages are supplied with food for other meals.

Charges: $46 per person per day (or $300 per week) for room and food.

Write: The Guest Master.

Directions: To get to Nova Nada by car from Yarmouth, take Route 1 or 101 to Route 340 (the Hebron/Ohio exit from 101). Turn right on 340 toward Ohio, and continue until you get to Carleton, where you will see a sign for Kemptville. Turn right and go all the way to Kemptville. At the white church at the center of the village, bear left, following the sign to North Kemptville. After three miles the pavement will end. Continue onto the dirt road. Bear right at the fork. Soon you'll cross an iron bridge. You have 1.9 miles to go before you turn right at the Nova Nada sign (not up in winter). Keep going for just over three miles until you reach the gate. Open it and drive in.

If you are using public transportation, Air Canada flies from Boston, Halifax, and Portland, Maine, to Yarmouth. There are ferries from Bar Harbor and Portland, Maine, to Yarmouth, and from St. John, New Brunswick, to Digby, where you can continue to Yarmouth by bus. Arrange in advance with the Guest Master to be met in Yarmouth.

History: A former hunting lodge, Nova Nada has been the home of a monastic community of men and women hermits since 1972.

Description: Nova Nada's log cabin hermitages are deep in the woods of tall white pines. Guests may relax in the comfortable library or on the deck that overlooks one of the three lakes on which they may paddle canoes and kayaks. There are paths among sixty-five acres of quiet wilderness. The closest neighbor is three miles away.

Special Note: Guests arrive and depart on Thursdays. Communal activities are scheduled for Wednesday, Friday, Saturday, and Sunday. Monday and Tuesday are days of solitude. Please contact Nova Nada in writing for more information.

Crieff Hills Community

R.R. #2
Puslinch, Ontario N0B 2J0

Telephone: (519) 824-7898.

Order: Crieff Hills Community (Presbyterian Church in Canada).

Accommodations: Up to one hundred guests in seven guest houses in twin and single rooms, some with private baths.

Meals: In some guest houses, meals are provided; in others, meals are self-catered.

Charges: $12.20 to $19.40 per person per day for room only. Meals are $28 per day per person.

Write or telephone: The Bookings Secretary.

Directions: Crieff Hills is three kilometers south of Highway 401, five kilometers west of Highway 6 (on Leslie Road), and ten kilometers east of Cambridge Townline Road (on Puslinch Road 1).

For those using public transportation, Airways transit has service from Toronto International Airport to Cambridge Holiday Inn. In addition, there are bus and train services to Guelph. Please contact the Bookings Secretary for more information.

History: Crieff is named after a town at the edge of the Scottish Highlands. Scots settled here in the 1830s to clear the land and build log cabins and barns. These in time gave way to stone houses. In the 1920s Col. John B. MacLean (founder of *MacLean's* magazine and the *Financial Post*) restored the church grounds, was given the old manse, and acquired adjacent land, which he named Crieff Hills Farm. When he died in 1950, he left this to the Presbyterian Church in Canada. The Reverend Robert Spencer began to develop the community and its property in the 1970s.

Description: Crieff Hills has 250 acres of rolling farmland with charming and picturesque old stone and wood buildings converted for use by the community and its guests today. Among these buildings are a squared log house (1838), a stone house (1872), a stone schoolhouse (1874), and a delightful old milk house (pictured here). Additional lodges have been constructed recently.

Points of Interest: Located in south central Ontario, Crieff Hills is within easy access to Niagra Falls and Toronto.

Holy Cross Priory

204 High Park Avenue
Toronto, Ontario M6P 2S6

Telephone: (416) 767-9081. (Best times to call: 8:00 A.M. to 12:00 noon and 5:30 P.M. to 6:30 P.M.)

Facsimile: (416) 767-4692.

Order: Order of the Holy Cross (Anglican Church of Canada).

Accommodations: Five guests in three single and one double room in the priory, all with shared baths.

Meals: Breakfast only. Other meals by special arrangement.

Charges: $40 per person per day for bed and breakfast. Additional meals are negotiable.

Write, telephone, or fax: The Prior.

Directions: Please contact the Prior for directions by car and by public transportation.

History: It was in 1884 that the Order of the Holy Cross was founded in New York City by an Episcopal priest, James Otis Sargent Huntington. The Order's earliest charitable works were on New York's Lower East Side. In the century plus following, the monks have spread across North America and ventured to West Africa. "In slum and suburb, rain forest and city, illiterate tribesmen and sophisticated Westerners alike have shared the word of God with the monks of Holy Cross." In 1973 the Order permanently settled in Toronto, moving to its present house in 1984.

Description: The priory is a very handsome three-story Queen Anne–style house complete with a wraparound porch with classical columns and a corner tower topped with a turret.

Points of Interest: Toronto, Canada's largest city and Ontario's Provincial capital, sits on the shores of Lake Ontario. The 1,800-foot-high CN Tower offers sweeping views of both lake and city. Closer to the ground, visitors may explore Toronto's religious, historical, and cultural points of interest. The city also has several professional sports teams.

> *And the Lord said unto Moses, "Make thee a fiery serpent, and set it upon a pole; and it shall come to pass, that everyone that is bitten, when he looketh upon it, shall live." And Moses made a serpent of brass, and put it upon a pole; and it came to pass, that if a serpent had bitten any man, when he beheld the serpent of brass, he lived.*
> —Numbers 21:8–9

> *And as Moses lifted up the serpent in the wilderness, even so must the Son of man be lifted up: That whosoever believeth in him should not perish, but have eternal life.*
> —John 3:14–15

St. John's Convent

One Botham Road
Willowdale, Ontario M2N 2J5

Telephone: (416) 226-2201.

Facsimile: (416) 222-4442.

Order: Sisterhood of St. John the Divine (Anglican Church of Canada).

Accommodations: Eighteen guests in the convent in single rooms with shared baths. There are also a twin room and a bed/sitting room, each with private bath.

Meals: Three meals daily.

Charges: Suggested rate of $40 per person per day for room and meals.

Write, telephone, or fax: The Guest Sister.

Directions: If driving from east or west, take Highway 401 to the Yonge Street exit and go north on Yonge Street to Florence Avenue (the first set of traffic lights). Go left (west) onto Florence Avenue, then left again (south) onto Botham Road. Botham Road jogs to the right on Franklin Avenue and then continues on to the convent grounds.

If using public transportation from Toronto, take the Yonge subway north to Sheppard Station. Then take a taxi to the convent or walk (fifteen minutes) south on Yonge Street, right on Florence Avenue, left on Botham Road, right on Franklin Avenue, and left again on to Botham Road and the convent.

History: The Sisterhood of St. John the Divine has the distinction of being the only Anglican religious order of women founded in Canada. It was begun in 1884 in Toronto. Sixty years later a permanent move was made to the present site in Willowdale. The sisterhood has worked in five Canadian provinces and today continues its ministries in Ontario and Alberta.

Points of Interest: Metropolitan Toronto offers many cultural attractions, including the Royal Ontario and other museums, the Casa Loma, the Ontario Parliament building, and the CN Tower.

Special Note: In addition to receiving individual guests, the convent offers group retreats. Please contact the Guest Sister for information.

Mount St. Mary's
Post Office Box 1147
Charlottetown, Prince Edward Island C1A 7M8

Telephone: (902) 892-6585. (Best time to call: 10:00 A.M. to 4:00 P.M.)

Facsimile: (902) 566-1832.

Order: Sisters of St. Martha (Roman Catholic).

Accommodations: Twelve guests: seven in single rooms in the motherhouse and four in single rooms in a neighboring house, all with shared baths; there is also one suite with private bath in the motherhouse.

Meals: Three meals daily.

Charges: $16.50 for room and $17.50 for meals per person per day.

Write, telephone, or fax: Sr. Marie Cahill.

Directions: If driving from New Brunswick, take the Confederation Bridge to Prince Edward Island. Once on the island, follow Route 1 to Charlottetown. Mount St. Mary's is on Mount Edward Road, which runs east of and parallel to Route 1.

For those using public transportation, the SMT bus service runs from St. John and Fredericton, New Brunswick, and from Halifax, Nova Scotia, to Charlottetown. If you are flying, Mount St. Mary's is five minutes from the airport. Guests may be met on arrival with prior arrangement. Cab service is also available.

History: The Prince Edward Island Sisters of St. Martha date back to 1916. In 1920, just four years after their foundation, the sisters acquired a frame farmhouse in Charlottetown. Named Mount St. Mary's, this became the community's motherhouse. The farmhouse was used until 1964, when the present handsome, contemporary, rambling red brick building was completed.

Description: Mount St. Mary's has forty-five acres of beautiful farmland, lawns, an orchard, and a cemetery. Guests may wish to walk along the trail where there was once a railroad track. The property borders the University of Prince Edward Island. Mount St. Mary's is within easy walking distance of downtown Charlottetown and shopping malls.

Points of Interest: Nicknamed Canada's "Garden on the Gulf," Prince Edward Island is the smallest of the provinces. Its low, rolling countryside, farms, and fishing villages all add to its charm and peaceful attraction. This is the setting of the popular book and television series, *Anne of Green Gables.* Charlottetown, the island's capital, is named for the wife of King George III. Here the Confederation Center for the Arts has three theaters, a library, an art gallery, and exhibition space. Also in the city is St. Dunstan's Basilica. Built in 1919 in flamboyant Gothic Revival style, the church has a cruciform floor plan. Visit Victoria Park for excellent harbor views. Venturing beyond the city limits, three distinctive drives are available to maximize your enjoyment of the island's tranquil beauty: Blue Heron Drive, King's Byway, and Lady Slipper Drive. Drop by the tourist information office (in the Shaw Building on Rochford Street) for maps and information.

Auberge de la Basilique

C.P. 57
Sainte-Anne-de Beaupré, Quebec G0A 3C0

Telephone: (418) 827-4475. (Best time to call: Monday through Friday 9:00 A.M. to 5:00 P.M.)

Facsimile: (418) 827-5162.

Order: Redemptorist Fathers (Roman Catholic).

Accommodations: 107 guests in the inn in single rooms, each with private bath.

Meals: Three meals daily in the cafeteria.

Charges: $46 per person per day for room.

Write, telephone, or fax: The Manager.

Directions: If driving from points west, take Autoroute 40 east to Beauport, then pick up either Route 138 or Route 360 east to Beaupré. Follow the sign to Sainte-Anne.

History: The history of the shrine goes back more than three centuries to 1658. During construction of the first church on this site, one of the construction workers was miraculously cured of lumbago. Ever growing in popularity, subsequent shrine churches were built in 1661, 1676, and 1876. The present basilica was built in 1923 and attracts a half million pilgrims and visitors annually.

Description: The Basilica Inn, designed to accommodate the large numbers of pilgrims who flock here, has a large lounge, a cafeteria, and a chapel. There is an elevator for the greater convenience of guests.

Points of Interest: The shrine basilica is a massive Romanesque-style stone church. On the facade, between the twin spires, is a gilt statue of St. Anne, the shrine's patroness and Mother of the Virgin. Visit the hillside behind the church with its Stations of the Cross. Nearby is the "Scala Santa," a re-creation of the Holy Stairs climbed by Jesus to meet Pontius Pilate. The shrine museum contains permanent exhibits regarding St. Anne, the history of the shrine, and religious art. West of Beaupré and farther down the St. Lawrence River are the spectacular Montmorency Falls and the city of Quebec, which is very picturesque and charming.

Abbaye Cistercienne d'Oka

1600 Chemin d'Oka
Oka, Quebec J0N 1E0

Telephone: (514) 479-8361.

Order: Cistercian (Trappist) monks (Roman Catholic).

Accommodations: Twenty-four men and four women in the guest house in single rooms, all with shared baths.

Meals: Three meals daily.

Charges: Freewill donations accepted.

Write or telephone: The Guest Master.

Directions: If driving from Montreal, take Highway 15 or Highway 13 north to 640 West and exit at Oka.

If using public transportation, take the Metro to Henri-Bourassa. Then take the bus for St. Eustache and transfer to the bus to Oka. Get off at La Trappe d'Oka.

History: The Cistercians are a reform within the Benedictine order dating back to medieval France. In the seventeenth century a further and more austere reform took place, centered at the Abbey of the Maison-Dieu Notre-Dame de la Trappe. Hence the popular name "Trappist." In 1881, seven monks from the Abbey of Bellefontaine, France, established this, the first Trappist monastery in Canada. The Abbaye d'Oka has, in turn, begun two other Canadian monasteries.

Description: The large and venerable abbey church is built of stone, as is the monastery. They are surrounded by fields and woodlands. The monks work in the orchard, vegetable gardens, and apiary.

Points of Interest: Oka is bordered by the Ottawa River on one side and the Laurentian Mountains on the other: ideal areas for quiet, reflective walks.

Abbaye Saint-Benoit-du-Lac

Saint-Benoit-du-Lac, Quebec J0B 2M0

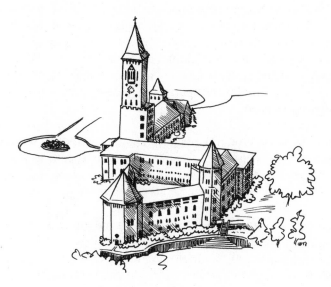

Telephone: (819) 843-4080. (Best times to call: 8:30 A.M. to 10:30 A.M. and 1:30 P.M. to 4:30 P.M.)

Facsimile: (819) 868-1861.

Order: Benedictine monks (Roman Catholic).

Accommodations: Thirty men and fifteen women in separate guest houses, each in a single room, and all with shared baths.

Meals: Three meals daily.

Charges: Available upon request.

Write, telephone, or fax: Men should contact the Père Hôtelier (Guest Master). Women should contact the villa (see Special Note below).

Directions: If driving from the New York or New England areas, take I-89 north from Burlington, Vermont, toward St. Albans to Route 105. Continue on 105 east to Richford. Then pick up Route 243 until it merges with Route 245. Continue on to Bolton Center. You will then see signs directing you to the abbey.

If driving from points east (Quebec city) or west (Montreal) on Autoroute 10, change to Route 112 and then pick up Route St.-Benoit just west of Magog. Continue south on Route St.-Benoit until you arrive in Austin, where there are signs directing you to the abbey.

If using public transportation, please contact the Guest Master for directions.

History: Monks from Normandy, France, arrived in southern Quebec in 1917 to found St. Benoit. Granted independent status in 1935, the present buildings were built starting in 1939. The architect was Dom Paul Bellot, a noted French monk and architect.

Description: The buildings at St.-Benoit can best be described as French Gothic Revival with strong borrowings from Moorish architecture. Throughout, dominant features include high-pitched roofs, lancet windows, and a permanent polychrome in brick and tile. Surrounding the massive abbey are the wonders of nature: a truly bucolic setting of thick forests (ablaze with color in autumn), fields where cattle graze, the serene Lake Memphremagog, and the mountains beyond.

The monks of St.-Benoit are known for their Gregorian chant, and they support themselves by producing cheeses and applesauce. Recordings of their singing, cheeses, applesauce, and other products are sold at the abbey shop.

Points of Interest: Montreal is 120 kilometers west of the abbey, offering cathedrals, churches, and other points of historic and cultural interest.

Special Note: Men guests are accommodated at the abbey guest house. (Hôtellerie Monastique). Women guests are also welcomed, but housed in a villa under the auspices of the Sisters of the Presentation of Mary at the following address:

Villa Ste.-Scholastique
Saint-Benoit-du-Lac, Quebec J0B 2M0

Abbaye Sainte-Marie-des Deux-Montagnes
2803 Chemin d'Oka
Ste.-Marthe-sur-le-Lac, Quebec J0N 1P0

Telephone: (514) 473-7278.

Order: Benedictine nuns (Roman Catholic).

Accommodations: Five women in three single and one twin room in the monastery, all with shared bath.

Meals: Three meals daily.

Charges: $30 per person per day for room and meals.

Write or telephone: The Guest Sister.

Directions: The abbey is thirty minutes from Montreal. If driving, take Autoroute 15 or 13 north to 640 west, then take Exit 8 to Duex-Montagnes (20th Avenue). On the Chemin d'Oka turn right and drive one mile.

For those using public transportation, there is air service to Mirabel and Dorval Airports. There is rail service from Central Station to the Duex-Montagnes city station. From the station there is taxi service to the abbey.

History: At the invitation of the Archbishop of Montreal, four nuns from the Monastery of Notre-Dame de Wisques, France, arrived in Canada in 1936 to begin this monastery. In ten years' time the monastery had grown so that it was raised to the status of an abbey, and the foundress, Mother Gertrude Adam, was solemnly blessed as first abbess. This is a monastery of the Congregation of Solesmes.

Description: The abbey, surrounded by fields and trees, is an extensive red brick building embellished with polychrome brickwork, towers, and spires. The architect was Edgar Courchesne, the Canadian disciple of Dom Paul Bellot, the "brick poet" who greatly influenced monastic and ecclesiastic architecture in Europe and America. A very traditional monastic community, the nuns have preserved the use of Latin Gregorian chant in the great abbey church, recordings of which may be purchased by mail or in their shop. The abbey has an excellent book bindery, and the nuns also make icons and produce cards and rosaries. "Being cloistered nuns with papal enclosure," they "wish to bear witness to the rich heritage from Solesmes and also share it with guests and visitors."

Points of Interest: The abbey is near the Lake "des Deux-Montagnes," named for the last two mountains of the Laurentians.

Les Recluses Missionnaires

12050 Boulevard Gouin Est
Montreal, Quebec H1C 1B8

Telephone: (514) 648-6801. (Best times to call: 8:00 A.M. to 11:00 A.M. and 12:00 noon to 4:30 P.M.)

Facsimile: (514) 643-1836.

Order: Les Recluses Missionnaires (Roman Catholic).

Accommodations: Twelve guests in the monastery in eight single and two twin-bedded rooms, two of which have private baths.

Meals: Three "ordinary, healthy, and complete meals" daily.

Charges: $30 per day for room and meals, single occupancy, and $35 per day for room and meals, double occupancy.

Write, telephone, or fax: Sister Cécile Viau, R.M.

Directions: Please contact Sister regarding directions by car or by public transportation.

History: To some extent both Montreal and Les Recluses Missionnaires share the same roots and history. Jacques Cartier, in his 1535 voyage, visited the Indian village of Hochelaga, climbed to the top of the mountain, and proclaimed it "un mont real." During the following century French men and women settled at Ville Marie near the same site not to trade, but to work as missionaries among the Indian population. One of the women, Jeanne LeBer, wishing to devote her life to prayer and solitude, lived as a hermit, first in a house and later in a wing attached to a convent chapel. Living in solitude for thirty-four years, she died in 1714. More than two centuries later, in 1942, two women, Rita Renaud and Jeanette Roy, in imitation of Jeanne LeBer, lived in seclusion and poverty. Joined by Jeanette Beaupre, they founded Les Recluses Missionnaires in 1943. The Montreal monastery was opened in 1950 at Rivière-des-Prairies. Today thirty sisters live in the Montreal monastery.

Points of Interest: As Montreal and Ville Marie were founded as a sacred city, there are many places of historic and religious interest in the area. The Church of Notre-Dame de Bon-Secours was built in 1772, the third church on the site. The city's cathedrals include Notre Dame (1829) in the Old City, Mary Queen of the World Cathedral (built in 1855 as a one-quarter-scale replica of St. Peter's Basilica in Rome, including interior baldachino), and the Anglican Christ Church Cathedral (English Gothic Revival style built in 1857). The largest and most visited of the churches is St. Joseph's Oratory. Rising more than 850 feet above sea level, the Oratory's immense dome dominates the city's skyline. The original chapel (1904), the founder's quarters, and the outdoor Stations of the Cross are also on the property of this magnificent shrine.

Special Note: The sisters offer "accommodations in the guest facilities of the monastery for anyone seeking a propitious place to meet the Lord in prayer, silence, and peace."

Par Lui, en Lui, Avec Lui

— The Sisters' motto

St. Peter's Abbey

Severin Hall Guestwing
Muenster, Saskatchewan S0K 2Y0

Telephone: (306) 682-1775.

Facsimile: (306) 682-1766.

Order: Benedictine monks (Roman Catholic).

Accommodations: Thirty guests in fifteen twin rooms in the guest wing, eight with private baths and seven with sink.

Meals: Three meals daily.

Charges: $35 for room and meals, single occupancy, and $40 for twin.

Write, telephone, or fax: The Guest Master.

Directions: The abbey is seventy miles east of Saskatoon on Highway 5.

For those using public transportation, the Saskatchewan Transportation Company (STC) has bus service twice daily from Saskatoon and from Regina.

History: Monks were among the first settlers in the area, arriving in 1903 to provide pastoral care to the German pioneers at St. Peter's Colony. Farming and printing (at first in German) were also some of the initial works of the monks. St. Peter's College was opened in 1921, and a new guest wing (Severin Hall) was completed in 1976.

Description: Severin Hall, the monastery, the college, and the abbey church (completed 1991) are a connecting complex of buildings. The extensive property includes a wooded area with trails. The open areas include farmland, grain fields, orchards, gardens, and parks. The rural setting provides a quiet place for prayer and reflection.

Points of Interest: One mile north of the abbey is St. Peter's Cathedral, which has many murals painted by the German artist Berthold Imhoff in 1919.

Special Note: "Guests are invited to share our food, work, and prayer."

Readership Response

for

A GUIDE TO MONASTIC GUEST HOUSES
Third Edition

Comments:

Optional: Name_____

Address _____

_____

Telephone _____

Thank you. Please mail to:

Robert J. Regalbuto, Author
c/o Morehouse Publishing
Post Office Box 1321
Harrisburg, PA 17105